MASTERING THE SOCIAL STUDIES MEAP TEST: GRADE 8

JAMES KILLORAN

STUART ZIMMER

MARK JARRETT

JARRETT PUBLISHING COMPANY

East Coast:
19 Cross Street
Ronkonkoma, NY 11779
(516) 981-4248

West Coast:
10 Folin Lane
Lafayette, CA 94549
(925) 906-9742

1-800-859-7679 FAX: (516) 588-4722

www.jarrettpub.com

Jarrett Publishing Company
19 Cross Street
Ronkonkoma, New York 11779

ISBN 1-882422-41-4

First Edition
Printed in the United States of America
by Malloy Lithographing, Inc., Ann Arbor, Michigan

10 9 8 7 6 5 4 3 2 1 01 00 99 98

ABOUT THE AUTHORS

James Killoran is a retired Assistant Principal. He has written *Government and You* and *Economics and You*. Mr. Killoran has extensive experience in test writing for the New York State Board of Regents in Social Studies and has served on the Committee for Testing of the National Council of Social Studies. His article on social studies testing has been published in *Social Education*, the country's leading social studies journal. In addition, Mr. Killoran has won a number of awards for outstanding teaching and curriculum development, including, "Outstanding Social Studies Teacher" and "Outstanding Social Studies Supervisor" in New York City. In 1993, he was awarded an Advanced Certificate for Teachers of Social Studies by the N.C.S.S.

Stuart Zimmer is a retired social studies teacher. He has written *Government and You* and *Economics and You*. He served as a test writer for the New York State Board of Regents in social studies and has written for the National Merit Scholarship Examination. In addition, he has published numerous articles on teaching and testing in social studies journals. He has presented many demonstrations and educational workshops at state and national teachers' conferences. In 1989, Mr. Zimmer's achievements were recognized by the New York State Legislature with a Special Legislative Resolution passed in his honor.

Mark Jarrett is a former social studies teacher and a practicing attorney at the San Francisco office of Baker and McKenzie, the world's largest law firm. Mr. Jarrett has served as a test writer for the New York State Board of Regents and has taught at Hofstra University. He was educated at Columbia University, the London School of Economics, the Law School of the University of California at Berkeley, and Stanford University, where he is a doctoral candidate in history. Mr. Jarrett has received several academic awards, including Order of the Coif at Berkeley and the David and Christina Phelps Harris Fellowship at Stanford University.

ALSO BY KILLORAN, ZIMMER AND JARRETT

Michigan: Its Land and Its People
Making Connections: Michigan and the Wider World
Mastering the Social Studies MEAP Test: Grade 5
The Key to Understanding Global History
The Key to Understanding U.S. History and Government
Mastering Global Studies
Mastering U.S. History and Government
Historia y gobierno de los Estados Unidos
Mastering Ohio's 9th Grade Citizenship Test
Mastering Ohio's 12th Grade Citizenship Test
Los Estados Unidos: su historia, su gobierno
Nuestro mundo: su historia, sus culturas
Ohio: Its Land and Its People
Ohio: Its Neighbors, Near and Far
Principios de economía
Texas: Its Land and Its People
New York: Its Land and Its People
North Carolina: The Tar Heel State

ACKNOWLEDGMENTS

The authors would like to thank the following Michigan educators who reviewed the manuscript, and whose comments, suggestions and recommendations proved invaluable:

Michael Yocum
Executive Director, Michigan Council for the Social Studies
Consultant to the Oakland County School District

Mel Miller
Social Studies Consultant
Macomb Intermediate School District
Clinton Township, Michigan

Cover design by Peter R. Fleck
Layout and typesetting by Maple Hill Press, Ltd., Huntington, NY
Maps and graphics by Morris Kantor and Computerized Cartography

This book is dedicated
...to my wife Donna and my children Christian, Carrie, and Jesse — *James Killoran*
...to my wife Joan and my children Todd and Ronald — *Stuart Zimmer*
...to my wife Goska and my children Alexander and Julia — *Mark Jarrett*

TABLE OF CONTENTS

UNIT 1: LAYING A FOUNDATION

UNIT 2: ANSWERING DIFFERENT TYPES OF QUESTIONS

UNIT 3: REVIEW OF CONTENT STANDARDS

UNIT 4: A PRACTICE TEST

PHOTO CREDITS

Cover: Michigan has more than 3,000 miles of shoreline bordering four of the five Great Lakes. This may explain why Michigan has more lighthouses than any other state in the nation. The lighthouse shown on the cover is a popular landmark known as "Big Red." It stands at the harbor entrance near Holland State Park in Holland, Michigan. © 1990 Gordon R. Gainer; The Stock Market, Inc.

CHAPTER 3 — DIFFERENT TYPES OF PROMPTS
Page 23: Library of Congress.

CHAPTER 6 — GEOGRAPHY
Page 48: United Nations.

CHAPTER 7 — HISTORY
Page 57: (t,m,b) Library of Congress; Page 59: (t,b) Library of Congress; Page 60: Library of Congress; Page 61: U.S Capital Historical Society; Page 62: Eastern National Park and Monument Association; Page 64: (t,b) Library of Congress; Page 65: Library of Congress; Page 66: (t, b) Library of Congress; Page 68: (t,b) Library of Congress; Page 69: Duke Homestead and Tobacco Museum, North Carolina; Page 74: Library of Congress.

CHAPTER 8 — ECONOMICS
Page 81: (t) United Nations, (m) National Archives, (b) Jarrett Archives; Page 83: (t, b) United Nations; Page 84: Jarrett Archives; Page 85: Jarrett Archives; Page 86: Jarrett Archives; Page 90: (t) Jarrett Archives, (b) Bureau of Engraving and Printing; Page 92: (b,r & b,l) Ford Motor Company; Page 93: National Archives; Page 94: (t,l) Japanese National Tourist Office, (t,r) Israeli Department of Tourism, (m,l) Japanese National Tourist Office, (m,r) Texas Department of Highways, (b,l) Indonesian Office of Tourism, (b,r) United Nations.

CHAPTER 9 — CIVICS
Page 101 (t) Library of Congress, (m) © S. Milstein, (b) Republican National Committee; Page 105: Library of Congress; Page 107: Collection of the U.S. Supreme Court; Page 109: (t) Library of Congress, (b) Schomberg Collection of the New York Public Library; Page 111: Republican National Committee; Page 112: United Nations; Page 115: Library of Congress; (t) National Archives, (b) U.S. Capitol Historical Society.

CHAPTER 11 — PUBLIC DISCOURSE AND DECISION-MAKING
Page 131: (t,m,b) Jarrett Archives; Page 133: Library of Congress.

CHAPTER 12 — A PRACTICE MEAP TEST IN SOCIAL STUDIES
Page 150: (1) Jarrett Archives, (2) United Nations, (3) Jarrett Archives, (4) Library of Congress, (5) Israeli Department of Tourism, (6) Pitlik Collection, (7) United Nations, (8) Jarrett Archives; Page 156: Library of Congress.

CHAPTER 1

WHAT LIES AHEAD

Taking tests is something that all students must do. Everyone wants to do well on the **Social Studies MEAP Test: Grade 8**. Unfortunately, just wanting to do well is not enough. You have to really work at it.

WHAT IS THE MEAP TEST?

The purpose of social studies is to prepare young people to become responsible citizens. In 1996, the Michigan Board of Education approved a new set of content standards in social studies, along with a plan to measure each student's educational development. This plan called for a statewide test in social studies. Knowledge of these content standards will be very important for achieving a good grade on the test.

On the Social Studies MEAP Test, you will be asked questions dealing with several major categories called **strands**:

STRANDS

- ✦ geography
- ✦ history
- ✦ economics
- ✦ civics
- ✦ inquiry
- ✦ public discourse and decision-making

CONTENT STANDARDS

These strands are divided into 22 **content standards**. Each content standard spells out what you are expected to know by the time you graduate from high school. The social studies content standards are listed on the following chart:

Social Studies Standards for the MEAP Test

STRANDS	***Historical Perspective***	***Geographic Perspective***	***Civic Perspective***	***Economic Perspective***	***Inquiry***	***Public Discourse and Decision-Making***
CONTENT STANDARDS	**I.1** *Time and Chronology*	**II.1** *People, Places and Cultures*	**III.1** *Purposes of Government*	**IV.1** *Individual and Household Choices*	**V.1** *Information Processing*	**VI.1** *Identifying and Analyzing Issues*
	I.2 *Comprehending the Past*	**II.2** *Human/ Environment Interaction*	**III.2** *Ideals of American Democracy*	**IV.2** *Business Choices*		**VI.2** *Persuasive Writing*
	I.3 *Analyzing and Interpreting the Past*	**II.3** *Location, Movement and Connections*	**III.3** *Democracy in Action*	**IV.3** *Role of Government*		
	I.4 *Judging Decisions from the Past*	**II.4** *Regions, Patterns and Processes*	**III.4** *American Government and Politics*	**IV.4** *Economic Systems*		
		II.5 *Global Issues and Events*	**III.5** *American Government and World Affairs*	**IV.5** *Trade*		

THE "BIG IDEAS" AND THEIR BENCHMARKS

Each of the content standards contains several "big ideas" or benchmarks, which explain specifically what you should know and what you should be able to do at various grade levels. The benchmarks are used to trace your progress at different times during your educational career.

For example, let's look at the eighth-grade benchmarks for the second content standard under the first strand, *Geographic Perspective.*

Strand: Geographic Perspective

Content Standard II.1:
Diversity of Peoples, Places, and Cultures

All students will describe, compare, and explain the locations and characteristics of places, cultures, and settlements.

Benchmarks. By eighth grade, students will:

- Locate and describe the diverse places, cultures, and communities of major world regions.
- Describe and compare characteristics of major world cultures including language, religion, belief systems, gender roles, and traditions.
- Explain why people live and work as they do in different regions.

The *content standards* give a general description of the "big ideas" in each strand. You will then be tested on your ability to do the specific things outlined in the *benchmarks.* For example, the second benchmark *(shown on the card above)* requires that you describe and compare the main characteristics of various major cultures, including their languages, religions, and traditions. This means you must have a general idea of where these cultures are located and know some of the characteristics of each culture.

To help you focus on what you must know and do for each benchmark, following each MEAP-type question in this book is the number of the benchmark being tested. In addition, at the end of each review chapter is a list of the benchmarks for the strand covered in that chapter.

THE TEST FORMAT

The questions on the eighth grade Social Studies MEAP Test all follow the same pattern.

They require you to know and understand the material listed in the benchmarks. You must also be able to apply this knowledge to interpreting a "prompt." A **prompt** is information presented in the question in the form of a reading, map, chart, graph, drawing, or other material. The prompt is used to activate your *prior knowledge* — what you already know in social studies. Thus, to do well on this test, you have to understand both:

- ✦ what you must know and do, according to the benchmarks, and
- ✦ how to analyze different types of prompts.

HOW THIS BOOK IS ORGANIZED

You will be responsible for knowledge you have learned from the sixth grade through the eighth grade. How can you be expected to remember so much information? With this book as your guide, you should find the test easier, and maybe even fun to take. ***Mastering The Social Studies MEAP Test: Grade 8*** will help you prepare to answer any type of question found on the test.

The following section-by-section review explains what you will find in this book.

UNIT 1: WHAT LIES AHEAD

This opening chapter, which you are reading, describes how the book is organized and introduces you to the eighth grade MEAP Test in Social Studies. **Chapter 2** gives you some powerful techniques for remembering important information, which will be helpful for the Social Studies MEAP Test and other tests as well.

UNIT 2: ANSWERING DIFFERENT TYPES OF QUESTIONS

This section of the book consists of three chapters. They focus on two of the three types of questions that appear on the MEAP Test. The third type of question, called an extended-response question, is covered in Chapter 11.

- **Chapter 3** deals with prompts. On the MEAP Test, each type of question begins with a prompt, which you must interpret.

- **Chapter 4** focuses on how to answer selected-response questions. In these questions, you will be asked to "select" the correct answer from a group of four possible choices.

- **Chapter 5** examines how to answer constructed-response questions. In these questions, you will be asked to perform a short task such as filling in a chart, creating a timeline, writing a paragraph, or completing a map.

UNIT 3: REVIEW OF THE CONTENT STRANDS

This section provides brief summaries of the information you need to review for each of the strands on the Social Studies MEAP Test. Each chapter contains a brief or capsule summary of the basic information you need to know for that strand. Each chapter also has a summary of the strand's "big ideas." It is followed by a series of practice questions. The chapter ends with a listing of that strand's benchmarks.

- **Chapter 6** reviews **geography**. It focuses on the physical and cultural geography of the world.

- **Chapter 7** reviews **history**. It summarizes the history of the United States from 1754 until 1815.

- **Chapter 8** reviews **economics**. It emphasizes the major terms and concepts of economics. It also compares our free market economic system with other economic systems around the world.

- **Chapter 9** reviews **civics**. It describes the American system of democratic government, including the structure of the federal government and state governments. It also reviews the rule of law and America's role in world affairs.

- **Chapter 10** reviews **inquiry**. This chapter will show you how to answer constructed-response questions on the inquiry section of the test.

- **Chapter 11** reviews **public discourse and decision-making**, including the "Core Democratic Values." The chapter shows you how to answer a sample extended-response question on a public policy issue, similar to the extended-response questions on the actual test.

UNIT 4: A PRACTICE TEST

The final section of this book contains a complete practice Social Studies MEAP Test. You should take this practice test under conditions similar to those of the actual test. This practice test will help increase your confidence and allow you to spot areas of weakness that need further review. You can go over the answers with your teacher in class as a final review before taking the actual MEAP Test.

By paying careful attention to your teachers at school, by completing your homework assignments, and by preparing with this book, you can be confident that you will do your best when the day of the real MEAP Test arrives.

CHAPTER 2

REMEMBERING IMPORTANT TERMS AND CONCEPTS

Have you ever watched workers building a house? You might have noticed that electricians, plumbers, bricklayers, and others use a variety of tools to help complete the job. Every good worker knows that the better the tools are, the better the work will be.

Like builders constructing a house, you need a good set of tools when you study. This chapter will supply you with some of these tools.

DEVELOPING VOCABULARY CARDS

Terms are words or phrases that refer to specific things. For example, the *Midwest* is a term. **Concepts** give a name to things that are not specific, such as general ideas or groups of things. *Democracy* is a concept. The Social Studies MEAP Test: Grade 8 will assess your knowledge of both terms and concepts.

One of the best ways to learn and remember a new term or concept is to create a vocabulary card. A **vocabulary card** is an index card on which you write important information about major terms and concepts.

To reinforce your learning, you should make vocabulary cards for the most important terms and concepts in each content area. The graphic organizers found in each content chapter of this book identify many of the terms and concepts you will need to know. Make a separate card for each one.

Each vocabulary card has two parts:

THE FRONT OF THE CARD

On the top line of the card, write the name of the term or concept. Below that line, define or explain it. Beneath the definition or explanation, provide an example, explain the importance of the term or concept, or give other important information about it. Use your textbook, school library, and the content summaries in this book to find the information you need to complete each card.

THE BACK OF THE CARD

On this side of the card, draw a picture that illustrates the term or concept. Your picture may show how something actually looks or may be symbolic. Turning the written information on the front of the card into an illustration on the back will help you to clarify the meaning of the term or concept. By illustrating the key points, you create a picture in your mind that will help you to remember the word or phrase.

Let's look at the term *Upper Peninsula*:

Front of card

UPPER PENINSULA

What is the Upper Peninsula?

Michigan is composed of two peninsulas: the Upper Peninsula and the Lower Peninsula. The Upper Peninsula is the more northern of the two. It is bordered by Lakes Superior, Michigan and Huron.

What are its main geographical features?

Forests, lakes and islands.

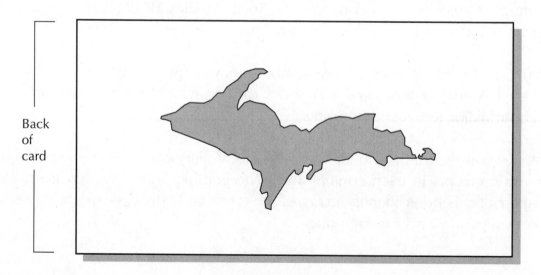

Back of card

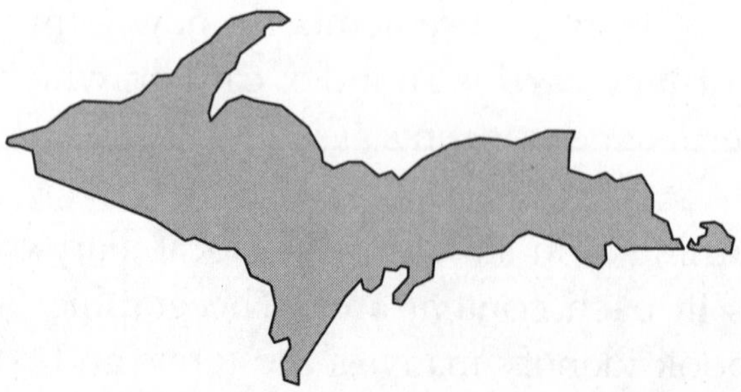

After you have completed a set of vocabulary cards, you can use them to help you prepare for the test.

- ✦ Look at the picture side of the card and try to recall the name of the term or concept.

- ✦ On the front of the card, look at the name of the term or concept. Try covering the rest of the card with your hand or a piece of paper. See how well you can recall the definition or example. Then remove your hand or the paper to see if you are correct.

USING MNEMONIC DEVICES

A very helpful tool for recalling factual information is a **mnemonic** (ne mon' ik) device. Mnemonic devices are word tricks that help you to remember information. They are especially useful when you have to memorize a list or group of items.

THE KEY WORD METHOD

To use this method, you take the *first letter* of each word on a list and arrange those letters to form a *new* word that is easy to remember. For example, a "key word" might be helpful for recalling the names of the five Great Lakes:

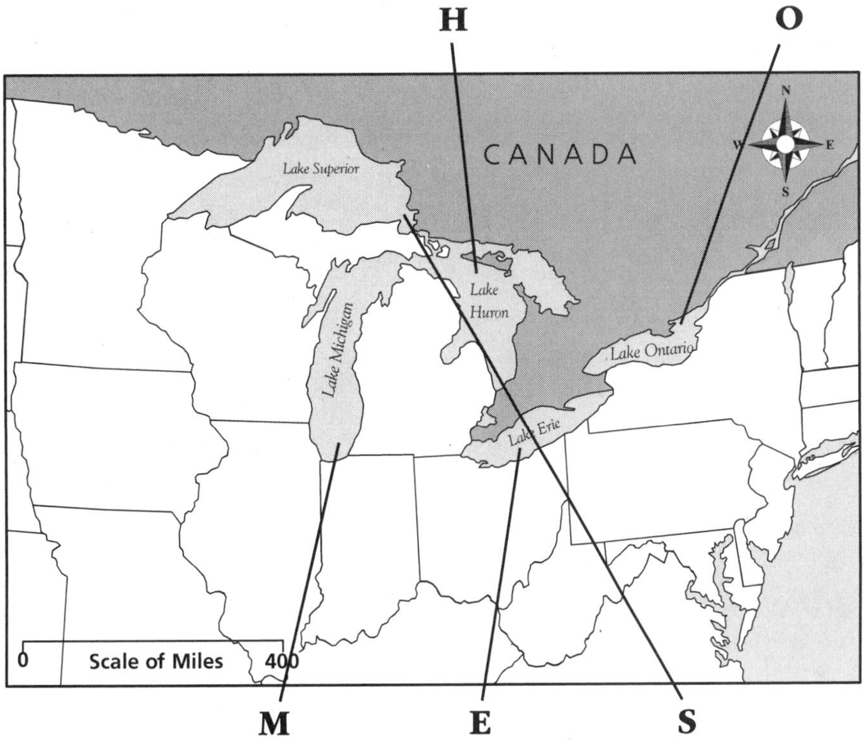

You can see that a handy key word for the names of the Great Lakes is **HOMES**. It uses the first letter in the name of each lake: **<u>H</u>**uron, **<u>O</u>**ntario, **<u>M</u>**ichigan, **<u>E</u>**rie, and **<u>S</u>**uperior.

THE KEY SENTENCE METHOD

Another mnemonic device is to create a "key sentence." For example, the flags of four nations flew over parts of Michigan at different times: France, Spain, England, and the United States. What would be an easy way to remember this group of nations?

1. Think of a word that rhymes with the name of each nation, or starts with the same letter or letters:

    - ✦ United States — Uncle (both words start with "Un")
    - ✦ France — Frank (both words start with "Fran")
    - ✦ Spain — speaks (both words start with "sp")
    - ✦ England — English (both words start with "Engl")

2. Now put these words together to form a sentence that will help you to remember the group of nations. For example:

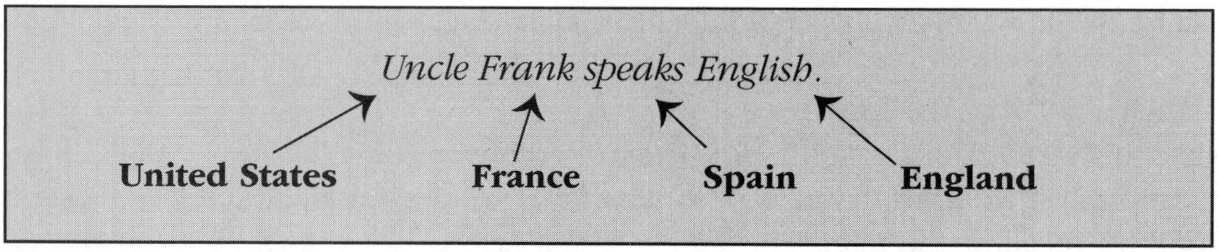

CHAPTER 3

DIFFERENT TYPES OF PROMPTS

On the Social Studies MEAP Test for Grade 8, there will be three types of questions:

- ✦ Selected-Response Questions
- ✦ Constructed-Response Questions
- ✦ Extended-Response Questions

Each of these types of questions will test your knowledge of social studies. The questions will ask you to apply your prior knowledge of social studies to interpreting a **prompt** *(a piece of data)*.

Each of the questions assumes that you know how to interpret the various prompts. You cannot begin to answer the questions unless you **understand the prompt.** In this chapter, you will examine the major types of prompts found on the test:

- Maps
- Bar Graphs
- Line Graphs
- Pie Charts
- Tables
- Timelines
- Drawings and Photographs
- Reading Selections

Our discussion of each prompt will be divided into three parts:

1. A description of the type of prompt.
2. An examination of each part of the prompt to help you interpret it.
3. Comprehension questions to check your understanding. (These questions will only test your ability to *interpret* prompts. They are not the same as MEAP Test questions, which are found throughout the rest of this book.)

MAPS

WHAT IS A MAP?

A map is a drawing of a geographic area. There are many kinds of maps. Some of the most common are:

- **Political maps**, showing the major boundaries between countries or states.
- **Physical maps**, showing the physical characteristics of a region, such as rivers, mountains, vegetation, and elevation *(height above sea level).*
- **Theme maps**, providing information on a theme such as natural resources, rainfall, languages spoken, average temperatures, or main points of interest.

STEPS TO UNDERSTANDING A MAP

1. Look at the Title. The title of the map tells you what kind of information is presented. For example, the title of the map below indicates it concerns the way land is used in the nation of Bangladesh.

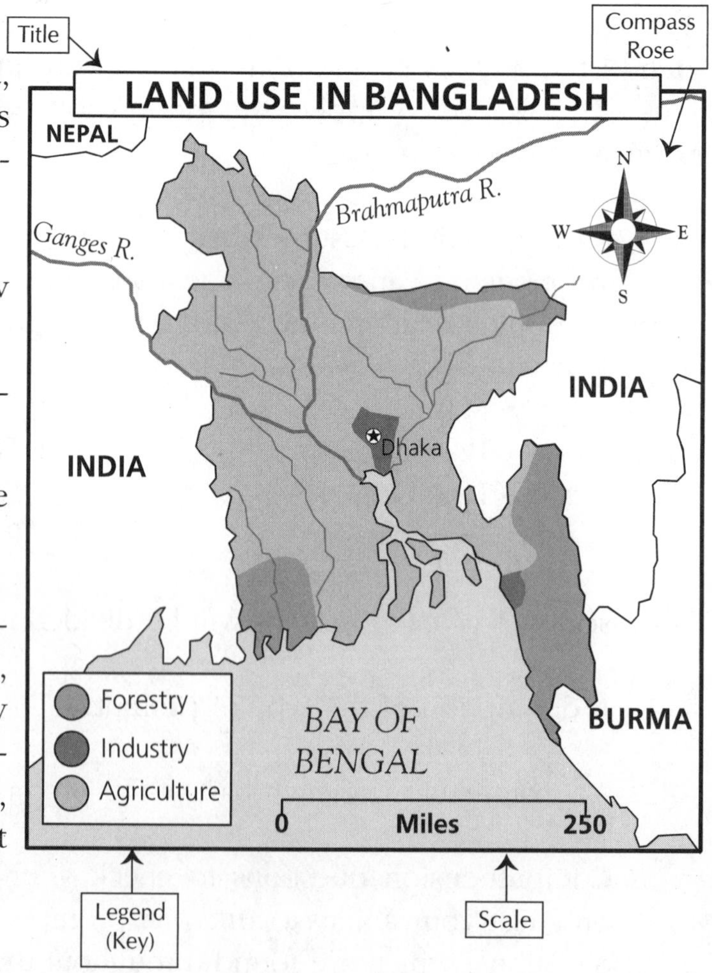

2. Look at the Legend. The legend, also called the **key**, lists the symbols used and identifies what they represent. In this map:

- the medium gray areas show where land is used for forestry;
- the dark gray areas show where industry is located;
- the light gray areas show where land is used for farming.

3. Look at the Compass Rose. It indicates the four basic directions: north, south, east, and west. Most maps show north at the top and south at the bottom. If no direction indicator appears, you can usually assume that north is at the top and south is at the bottom.

4. Look at the Scale. A map would be impossible to use if it were the same size as the area it shows. Mapmakers reduce the size so that it can fit onto a page. The scale indicates the actual distance between places on the map. The distance is usually shown in miles (or kilometers). For example, on one map an inch may represent 1 mile, while on another map an inch may represent 100 miles.

Finding Specific Information. To find specific information, you must use the legend and other map features together. For example, if you wanted to find which areas of Bangladesh are the most industrialized, here is what you must do:

1. In the map legend on page 11, notice that *dark gray* indicates areas that have industry. Look for areas in dark gray on the map.

2. Small sections in both the central and southeastern parts of Bangladesh are shown in dark gray, indicating that these areas are where industries are located.

INTERPRETING A MAP

Now answer the following questions about the map on the previous page.

CHECKING YOUR UNDERSTANDING

What is most of the land in Bangladesh used for? ______________________

Based on the information on the map, what are some major occupations you might expect to find in Bangladesh? ______________________

____

BAR GRAPHS

WHAT IS A BAR GRAPH?

A bar graph is a chart made up of parallel bars of different lengths. A bar graph is often used to compare two or more things, and how they have changed over time.

Name______________________ Teacher______________________

Steps to Understanding a Bar Graph

1. Look at the Title. The title tells you the topic of the graph. For example, the title of the following bar graph indicates that the graph shows where immigrants to the United States came from, between 1900 and 1995.

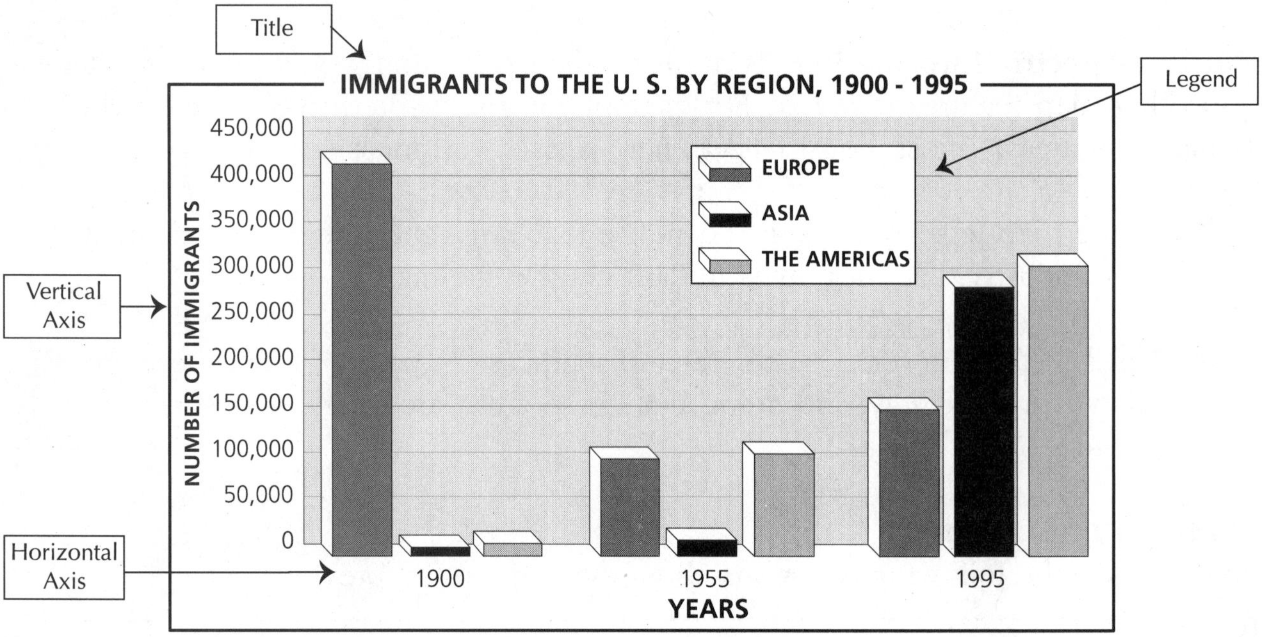

2. Look at the Legend. It shows what each bar represents. In the graph above:

- the dark gray bars represent Europe
- the black bars represent Asia
- the light gray bars represent the Americas (North, Central, and South America)

3. Look at the Vertical and the Horizontal Axis.

- The **vertical axis** runs from top to bottom. It usually measures the length of the bars. Here, it lists the number of immigrants — from 0 to 450,000.

- The **horizontal axis** runs from left to right. Here the horizontal axis indicates the years being compared: 1900, 1955, and 1995.

Note: Some bar graphs show bars running sideways. The only difference between an up-and-down bar graph and a sideways one is that the axes are reversed.

Finding Specific Information. To find specific information, you must examine the features of the bar graph closely. For example, to find out how many immigrants came to the United States from Europe in 1900, here is what to do:

1. On the horizontal axis, find the year 1900.

2. Choose the bar that represents Europe. According to the legend, this is the dark gray bar.

3. Run your finger to the top of the bar, and slide it slightly to the left. When you reach the vertical axis, you will find it is between 400,000 and 450,000. This shows that the number of immigrants from Europe in 1900 was about 425,000.

INTERPRETING A BAR GRAPH

Now that you have read about bar graphs, answer the following questions about the bar graph on the previous page.

CHECKING YOUR UNDERSTANDING

In which year — 1900, 1955, or 1995 — did the least number of Europeans come to the United States? ______________________

How many immigrants came to the United States from Asia in 1955?

____

LINE GRAPHS

What Is a Line Graph?

A line graph is a chart composed of a series of points connected by a line. A line graph is often used to show how something has changed over a period of time.

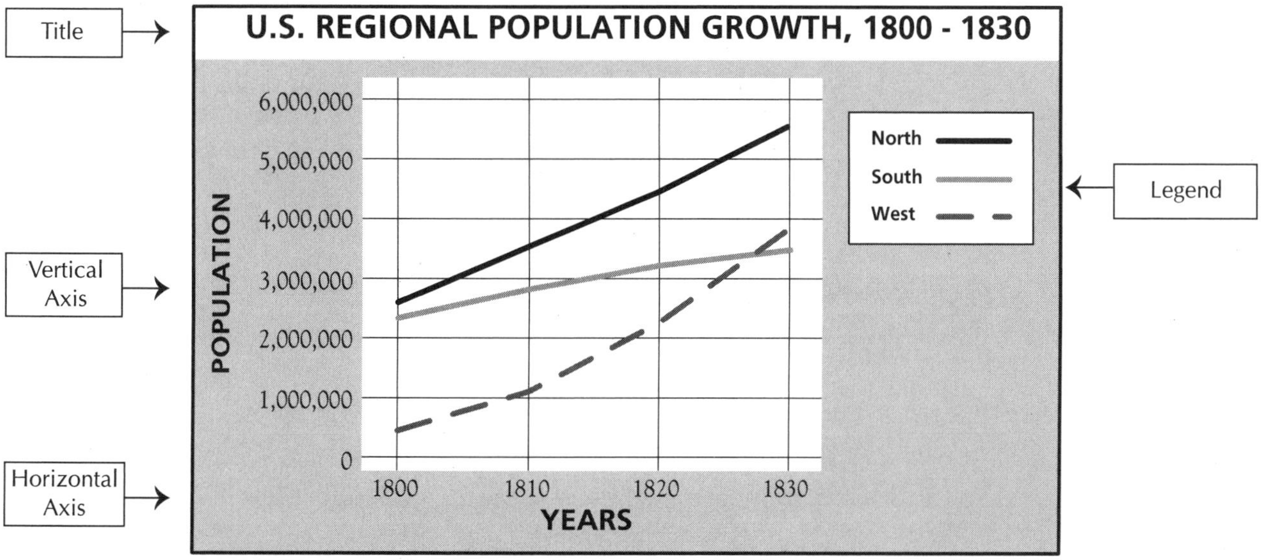

Name______________________ Teacher______________________

STEPS TO UNDERSTANDING A LINE GRAPH

1. Look at the Title. The title tells you the topic of the graph. In the graph on the previous page, the title indicates that this line graph compares regional population growth in the United States between 1800 and 1830.

2. Look at the Vertical Axis and the Horizontal Axis.

- The **vertical axis** runs from bottom to top. It often measures the size of something. As you move up the vertical axis, the numbers get larger. Note that the vertical axis in this line graph shows the population in millions.

- The **horizontal axis** runs from left to right. In this line graph, the horizontal axis shows years. The first year is 1800, and the dates continue in ten-year intervals until 1830.

3. Look at the Legend. If there is a legend, it explains what each line represents. If a graph has only one or two lines, there is often no legend because the information is marked directly on the graph. If a graph has more lines, however, a legend is often needed. In this graph, the legend tell us that the **black** line indicates the **North's population**, the **gray** line indicates the **South's population**, and the **dashed** line indicates the **West's population**.

Finding Specific Information. For specific information, you must examine the two axes. For example, what was the North's population in the year 1820?

- First, run your finger across the horizontal axis until you reach the year 1820.

- Now move your finger up until you reach the line representing the North. To find the actual number, slide your finger to the left until you reach the numbers on the vertical axis. This point intersects about midway between the "4,000,000" and the "5,000,000" line.

- Thus, the North's population in the year 1820 was about 4,500,000 people.

INTERPRETING A LINE GRAPH

Now answer the following questions about the line graph on the previous page.

CHECKING YOUR UNDERSTANDING

What was the difference in population between the South and West in 1800?

____

In which section of the nation was population rising fastest? ______________

____

PIE CHARTS

WHAT IS A PIE CHART?

A pie chart, also called a circle graph, is a circle divided into sections of different sizes. A pie chart is often used to show the relationship between a whole and its parts. When two pie charts are presented together, as in the example below, you can quickly compare relationships between years.

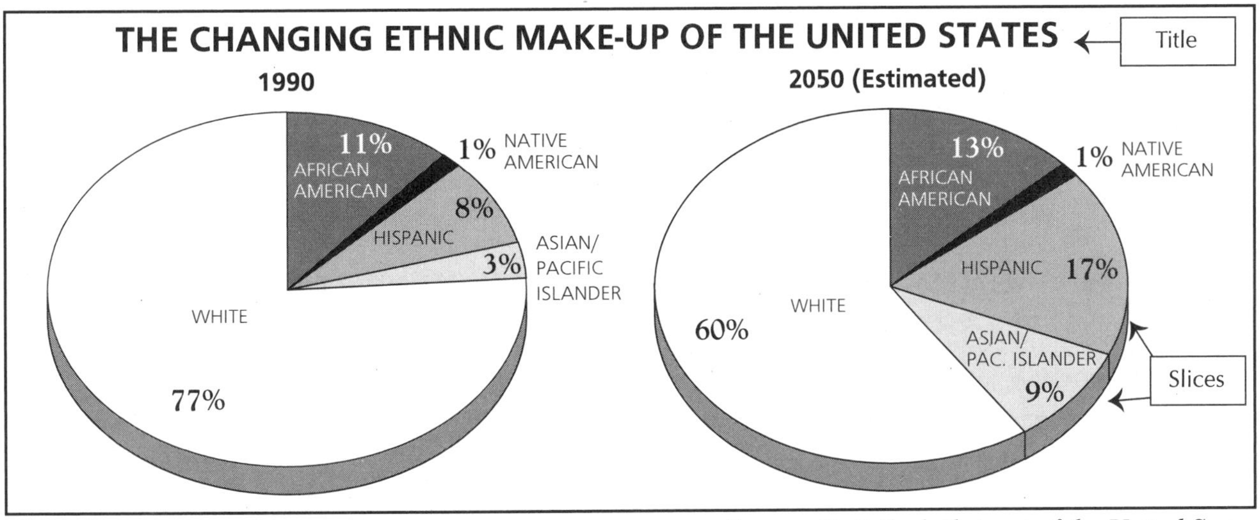

Source: Statistical Abstract of the United States

STEPS TO UNDERSTANDING A PIE CHART

1. Look at the Title. The title tells you the topic. For example, these pie charts show the ethnic make-up of the U.S. in 1990 and the estimated ethnic makeup in 2050.

2. Look at the Slices. Each slice shows its size or relationship to the whole pie. Think of the pie as 100% of something. If you add up all the slices, they total 100%. In each of these two pies, five different ethnic groups that make up the U.S. population are named on the pie slices.

3. Look at the Legend. Sometimes a pie chart has a legend showing what each slice of the pie represents. If the information is shown on the slices, a legend is not needed.

Finding Specific Information

To find specific information, examine each slice. For example, to find out what percentage of the U.S. population was made up of African Americans in 1990, look for the slice marked "African Americans" in the chart marked "1990." It was 11% of the total.

INTERPRETING A PIE CHART

Now answer the following questions about the pie charts on the previous page.

CHECKING YOUR UNDERSTANDING

Which group is expected to increase the most between 1990 and 2050?

____

Which group is expected to be the same percentage in 2050 as in 1990?

____

TABLES

What Is a Table?

A table is an arrangement of words or numbers in columns and rows. A table is often used to organize large amounts of information so that individual facts can be easily located and compared.

Title

Column Headings (Categories)

Rows

ESTIMATED AFRICAN-AMERICAN POPULATION IN THE THIRTEEN BRITISH COLONIES, 1690-1750

Year	New England Colonies	Middle Colonies	Southern Colonies
1690	905	2,472	13,307
1700	1,680	3,361	22,476
1710	2,585	6,218	36,063
1720	3,956	10,825	54,058
1730	6,118	11,683	73,220
1740	8,541	16,452	125,031
1750	10,982	20,736	204,702

Source: *Historical Statistics of the United States*

Name______________________________ Teacher______________________________

STEPS TO UNDERSTANDING A TABLE

1. Look at the Title. The title states the overall topic. For example, the table on the previous page provides information about the number of African Americans living in the thirteen British colonies of North America, from 1690 through 1750.

2. Look at the Categories. Each table has various categories of information. These categories are named in the **column headings** across the top of the table. In this table, there are four different categories: *Year, New England Colonies, Middle Colonies,* and *Southern Colonies.* The **rows** contain information for each category.

Finding Specific Information

For specific information, you must find where the **columns** and **rows** intersect. For example, if you want to know the total number of African Americans living in the Middle Colonies in 1730, here is what you must do:

- Put your right index finger on the column marked *Middle Colonies.* This column shows the African-American population in the Middle Colonies for various years.

- Put your left index finger on the column marked *Year.* Slide your finger down until it reaches the row for the year *"1730."*

- Slide your right finger down the *Middle Colonies* column to the *"1730"* row. You can see that the total number of African Americans living in the Middle Colonies in 1730 was 11,683.

INTERPRETING A TABLE

Now answer the following questions about the table on the previous page.

CHECKING YOUR UNDERSTANDING

What was the total number of African Americans living in the thirteen British colonies in 1740?

____

Which section had the largest number of African Americans in 1750: the New England Colonies, the Middle Colonies, or the Southern Colonies?

____

Name______________________ Teacher______________________

TIMELINES

WHAT IS A TIMELINE?

A timeline shows a group of events arranged in chronological order along a line. **Chronological order** is the order in which these events occurred. The first event to occur is the first event to appear on the timeline. The span of a timeline can be anything from a short period to several thousand years. The main function of a timeline is to show how events are related to each other. Timelines can be made horizontally or vertically, and you may see either kind on the MEAP Test.

Title →	FROM REVOLUTION TO NATIONHOOD: AMERICA FROM 1775 TO 1791					
Dates →	1775	1776	1781	1786	1787	1791
Events →	First shots fired between British and colonists; Revolutionary War begins	Thomas Paine writes *Common Sense*; Declaration of Independence issued	Articles of Confederation go into effect	Shays' Rebellion put down	Constitutional Convention meets in Philadelphia	Bill of Rights ratified by the states

STEPS TO UNDERSTANDING A TIMELINE

1. Look at the Title. The title tells you the general topic. In the sample above the title indicates that the timeline lists important events or "milestones" in our country's history from the start of the American Revolution through 1791.

2. Look at the Events. Events on the timeline are related to the title. For example, in this timeline each event was a major development in the transition from British colonies to nationhood.

3. Look at the Dates. Events are placed on the timeline in chronological order. A timeline is always based on a particular time period, no matter how brief or long. For example, this timeline starts in the later part of the 1700s and continues almost to the beginning of the 1800s.

The space between events is proportional to the actual time that has passed. If you were to add another event, its date might fall between two existing dates on the timeline. For example, if you wanted to add the Treaty of Paris in 1783 that ended the Revolutionary War, where would it go? Since 1783 is closer to 1781 *(2 years)* than it is to 1786 *(3 years)*, you would place it on the timeline slightly closer to 1781 than to 1786.

4. Be Aware of Special Terms. To understand questions about timelines or time periods, you should be familiar with two special terms:

- ✦ A **decade** is a ten-year period.
- ✦ A **century** is a 100-year period.

> **Note:** Identifying centuries may seem confusing at first. For example, the 20th century refers to the 100 years from 1901 to 2000. This numbering system came about because we start counting from the year it is believed that Christ was born. Thus, the first one hundred years after the birth of Christ were the years 1-100. This is called the **first century**. The second century went from 101 to 200; the third century was from 201 to 300, and so on.

5. Look at the Passage of Time. Remember that events are arranged from the earliest event (on the left) to the most recent event (on the right). To measure the number of years from one date to another, subtract the smaller date from the larger date. If it is the year 1999, how long has it been since Michigan was admitted as a state in 1837? By subtracting 1837 from 1999, we find that it was 162 years ago:

1999 *(assume this is the current year)*
\- 1837 *(the year Michigan was admitted as a state)*
162 years ago

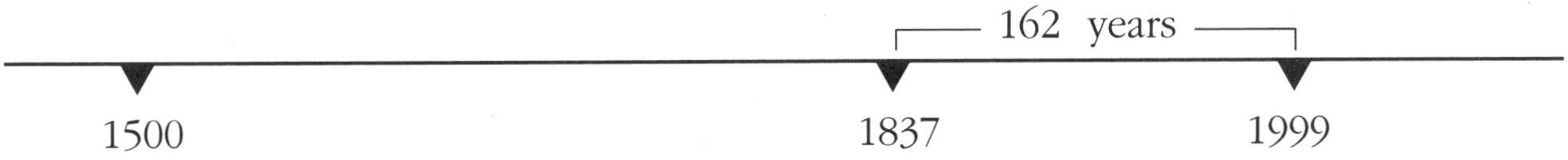

INTERPRETING A TIMELINE

Now answer the following questions about the special terms related to timelines, and the timeline on page 20.

CHECKING YOUR UNDERSTANDING

Which century includes the years 1801-1900? ____________________

What will the next century, 2001-2100, be called? ____________________

On what time period does the timeline focus? ____________________

How many years are covered by the timeline? ____________________

Which event happened first: the effective date of the Articles of Confederation, or the start of the American Revolution? ____________________

Name____________________ Teacher____________________

Creating a Timeline

Let's put your understanding of timelines to work. Below is a list of events and when they occurred. Use this information to create a timeline.

1803: Purchase of the Louisiana Territory
1775: Fighting at Lexington and Concord begins
1812: War breaks out with Great Britain
1791: The Bill of Rights is adopted
1787: The Northwest Ordinance is passed
1808: James Madison is elected President

Use the graphic below to create your timeline:

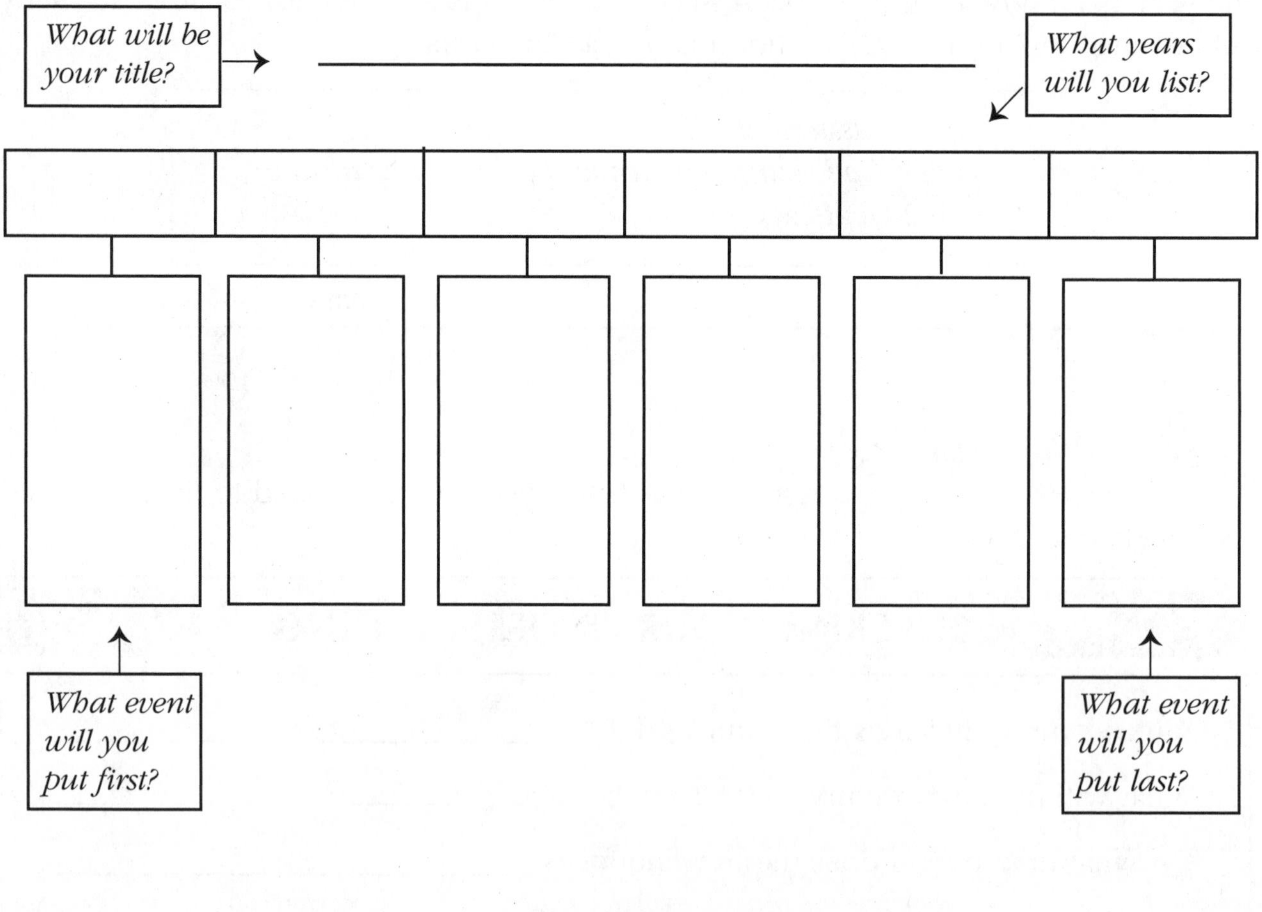
What will be your title?
What years will you list?
What event will you put first?
What event will you put last?

Name______________________ Teacher______________________

DRAWINGS AND PHOTOGRAPHS

WHAT IS A DRAWING OR PHOTOGRAPH?

A drawing or photograph shows how something looked in the past or looks today. Drawings and photographs are especially useful for understanding the past by showing how people looked and dressed, and what they once did.

Often, a photograph allows us to get the "feeling" of an earlier period of time or a different place. Since photography was not invented until the mid-1800s, we rely on artists' drawings and paintings to show what things looked like before that time.

Children after a day of work in a coal mine in 1870

STEPS TO UNDERSTANDING A DRAWING OR PHOTOGRAPH

1. Look at the Title or Caption. Most drawings or photographs have a title or caption that identifies what is being shown. For example, in this photograph the caption is *Children after a day of work in a coal mine in 1870.*

2. Look at the Details. To find specific information, examine the *details* in the photograph or drawing. For example, if you want to know what child labor was like for some children in the 1870s, here is what to do:

- Look carefully at the physical details and consider what they might mean. For example, the boys in this picture are probably 10 to 12 years old. All of them are wearing hats, coveralls, and heavy gloves. Their faces are dirty. They don't look very healthy. None of the children are smiling — unusual for such a large group of boys.

- Based on this photograph, it seems clear that in the 1870s one group of people who worked in coal mines were young boys. Eventually, laws were passed in the early 1900s that prevented the use of child labor in the United States.

Interpreting a Drawing or Photograph

Now that you have looked at the details, answer the following questions based on the photograph on the previous page.

CHECKING YOUR UNDERSTANDING

Do you think these boys enjoyed their work? ______________________

Explain. ______________________

____

Do you think these children attended school? ______________________

Explain. ______________________

____

What jobs do you think these boys did in the mine? ______________________

____

____

Name______________________ Teacher______________________

READING SELECTIONS

WHAT IS A READING SELECTION?

A reading selection consists of a statement or a group of statements about a particular topic or subject. It may be a brief quotation or a short paragraph. The main function of the selection is to present someone's ideas about a topic.

STEPS TO UNDERSTANDING A READING SELECTION

To better understand a reading selection you should note that the writer presents a series of facts to prove a point. Ask yourself the following questions about each reading selection:

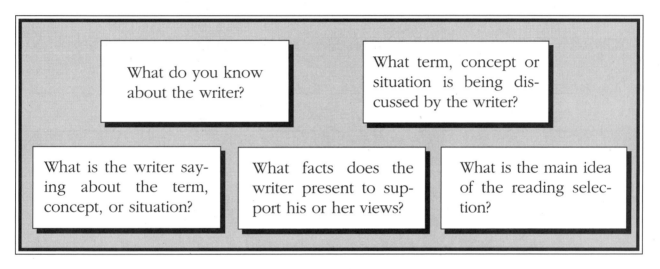

- What do you know about the writer?
- What term, concept or situation is being discussed by the writer?
- What is the writer saying about the term, concept, or situation?
- What facts does the writer present to support his or her views?
- What is the main idea of the reading selection?

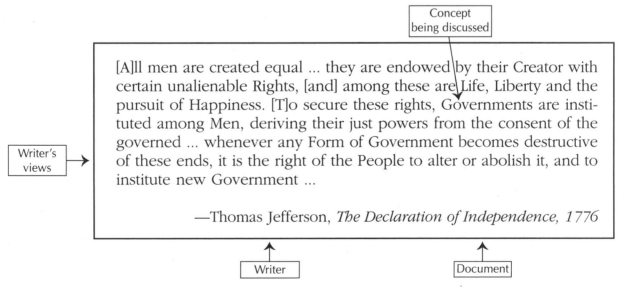

Concept being discussed

Writer's views

> [A]ll men are created equal ... they are endowed by their Creator with certain unalienable Rights, [and] among these are Life, Liberty and the pursuit of Happiness. [T]o secure these rights, Governments are instituted among Men, deriving their just powers from the consent of the governed ... whenever any Form of Government becomes destructive of these ends, it is the right of the People to alter or abolish it, and to institute new Government ...
>
> —Thomas Jefferson, *The Declaration of Independence, 1776*

Writer

Document

INTERPRETING A READING SELECTION

Now answer the following questions about the reading selection on page 25.

CHECKING YOUR UNDERSTANDING

What is the main idea of the selection? ______________________________

____

____

Why were the words in this reading passage important to the future of the United States? ____

____

____

Name______________________ Teacher______________________

CHAPTER 4

ANSWERING SELECTED-RESPONSE QUESTIONS

There will be three types of questions on the MEAP Test: selected, constructed, and extended-response questions. This chapter examines **selected-response** questions.

THE STRUCTURE OF THE QUESTION

Selected-response questions consist of a prompt followed by a cluster of five multiple-choice questions. You will first be asked to read and study the prompt. Then for each question, you will need to select the best answer from among four possible choices.

WHAT IS BEING TESTED?

In selected-response questions, you are being tested on **two** things:

- **Understanding the Prompts.** The prompt on which these questions are based will vary. It could be a short reading, a map, a chart, a graph, a drawing, a photograph, or a combination of these. In this chapter we assume that you know how to read and analyze the prompt. (Chapter 3 has already focused on interpreting prompts.)

- **Understanding the Benchmarks.** It will not be enough to just interpret the prompt, because the test questions will ask you to go one step further. You will also need to use your prior social studies knowledge to choose the correct answer. This prior knowledge will be based on your mastery of the **benchmarks** of Michigan's curriculum for eighth grade social studies.

> **REMEMBER:** You will **NOT** be able to answer the questions just from your understanding of the prompt. You will have to use both the prompt and your knowledge of the social studies **benchmarks**.

A SAMPLE SELECTED-RESPONSE QUESTION

Let's take a look at a typical selected-response question that you might find on the Social Studies MEAP Test for Grade 8. The following question tests your ability to read a map and your prior background knowledge of world regions and cultures.

Directions: Examine the following map and use it with what you already know to answer the questions that follow.

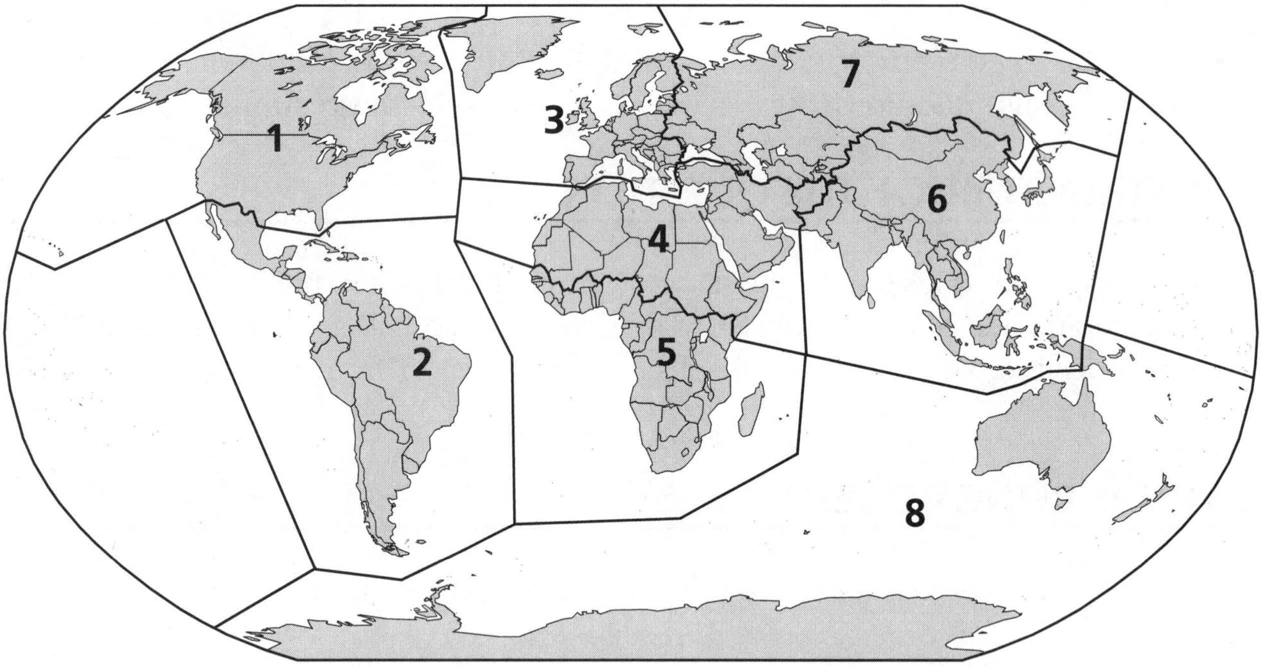

1 Which statement about Region 6 is accurate?

A It has the largest number of people.
B It has the world's largest oil reserves.
C It is the birthplace of Judaism, Christianity, and Islam.
D It is home to the world's largest rain forest.

2 In which region of the world would you expect to find both the world's largest desert and the world's longest river?

A Region 2 **C** Region 5
B Region 4 **D** Region 6

3 In which region would you expect to find the lowest population density?

A Region 4 **C** Region 6
B Region 5 **D** Region 8

Name ______________________ Teacher ______________________

4 Which occupations are MOST commonly found in Region 2?

A iron mining and camel herding
B rice farming and high tech manufacturing
C coffee growing and copper mining
D gold mining and growing tea

5 Which statement about Region 6 is accurate?

A It has some advanced industrial nations, specializing in car manufacturing, high technology, and communications equipment.
B Most of its people live in mountainous areas and speak Swahili.
C The principal spoken language is Arabic, and most people are followers of Islam.
D It was the home of the great Maya, Aztec, and Inca civilizations.

EXPLANATION OF ANSWERS

1 Which statement about Region 6 is accurate?

The answer is **A.** Region 6 contains two of the most populous nations in the world: China and India. Other nations in this region, like Bangladesh, Japan, and Indonesia, are also heavily populated. Region 6 has as many people as all the other regions of the world combined. Therefore, it is the most populated region. None of the other statements apply to Region 6. For example, the world's largest rain forest is located in South America (Region 2). This question tests your ability to describe major patterns of world population. The benchmark tested here is II.4.MS.3.*

2 In which region of the world would you expect to find both the world's largest desert and the world's longest river?

The answer is **B.** This question tests your ability to locate and describe the major physical features of the world. The Sahara Desert is the world's largest desert and the Nile, over 4,000 miles long, is the world's longest river. Both of these are located in Region 4, the Middle East and North Africa. This question tests your ability to locate major physical features in the world. The benchmark tested here is II.4.MS.3.*

* The benchmarks for each subject are listed at the end of each content chapter.

Name ______________________________ Teacher ______________________________

3 In which region would you expect to find the lowest population density?

The answer is **D.** Using the map as a guide, you may realize that although Australia and Antarctica (Region 8) occupy about 15% of the world's land area, they are the least inhabited continents in the world. This question tests your ability to describe the consequences of human/environment interactions in several different types of environments. The benchmark tested here is II.2.MS.3.

4 Which occupations are MOST commonly found in Region 2?

The answer is **C.** You should realize that Region 2, South America, is known for its coffee (Colombia and Brazil) and copper mines (Chile). None of the other pairs of occupations are accurate about Region 2. For example, the cultivation of rice and high technology are occupations often found in Asia (Region 6). The question tests your ability to locate and describe some common occupations of major world regions. The benchmark tested here is II.3.MS.1.

5 Which statement about Region 6 is accurate?

The answer is **A.** You should realize that nations bordering the Pacific Ocean in Region 6, such as South Korea, Taiwan, Japan, Singapore, and China are industrialized, high-techology areas. Their economic growth rates have been consistently increasing in recent years. None of the other statements apply to Asia. This question also tests your ability to locate and describe characteristics of major regions of the world. The benchmark tested here is II.2.MS.1.

CHAPTER 5

ANSWERING CONSTRUCTED-RESPONSE QUESTIONS

Unlike selected-response questions in which you *select* an answer from a list of choices, **constructed-response questions** require you to *create* your own answer to a question or a series of questions. Like selected-response questions, this type of question tests your understanding of the "big ideas." There are five constructed-response questions on the 8th grade Social Studies MEAP Test — one for each strand: geography, history, economics, civics, and inquiry.

THE "ACTION WORDS"

Many constructed-response questions will ask you to write something. For example, they may ask you to identify and explain the consequences of something, to identify reasons to support or reject something, or to classify positive or negative effects. What each question specifically requires you to write about will be stated in the "**action words**" of the question. Following are some of the most common action words and hints on how to respond to them.

✦ **IDENTIFY**

Identify means to **name** or give the distinguishing characteristics of something. It is generally used when you name one or more places, people, or things.

- **Sample Question:** *Identify* two U.S. presidents before the War of 1812.

- **Hint:** To identify something is to name it or give its distinguishing features. You do not have to explain it further.

- **Model Answer:**

Two presidents of the United States before the War of 1812 were George Washington and Thomas Jefferson.

✦ DESCRIBE

Describe means to **tell about** something.

- **Sample Question**: *Describe* the Islamic religion.

- **Hints**: To describe something is usually to tell about the *what*, *who*, *when*, and *where*. Start by answering the *what* first. Try to draw a word picture of *what* you are describing. Then answer the *who*, *when,* and *where* if they apply.

- **Model Answer**:

Islam is a major world religion that was founded by Mohammed in the Middle East around 600 A.D. Muslims believe in one God, Allah, and that Mohammed was his prophet.

Often on the MEAP Test you will be asked to describe something you have identified.

- **Sample Question**: *Identify* and *describe* a major international organization.

- **Model Answer**:

One major international organization is the United Nations. The United Nations was created by the countries of the world in 1945 to help maintain peace while encouraging friendship and cooperation among nations. Today, its membership totals more than 180 countries, including almost every nation in the world. United Nations headquarters are located in New York City.

✦ EXPLAIN AND SHOW

Explain and **show** are often linked to the additional word *how* or *why*. Sometimes these instructions are even used interchangeably. The key in approaching any question with these particular "action words" is to determine whether it asks you to give an answer for *how* something happened or *why* it happened.

EXPLAIN AND SHOW HOW

In this type of question, the phrase "explain how" or "show how" is followed by a general statement. The general statement may ask you to explain "how" something works or "how" it relates to something else. Often, you are asked to present the parts that make a whole. Answering a "show" question is like painting a picture that displays different parts.

- **Sample Question**: *Explain how* the U.S. Constitution limits the power of our central government.

- **Hints**: You are expected to provide facts and examples that demonstrate how the general statement is true.

- **Model Answer**:

The U.S. Constitution contains provisions that limit the power of the federal government. The first ten amendments to the U.S. Constitution, called the Bill of Rights, states that individuals have certain rights that the federal government cannot take away. For example, an individual has the right to a speedy and public trial.

Explain and Show Why

Explain why or *show why* questions generally focus on causes. To *explain why* means to give one or more reasons why an event took place or to *show why* a relationship identified in the question occurred.

- **Sample Question**: At the Constitutional Convention, delegates from the larger states proposed that all states should be represented in the new federal government in proportion to their population. *Explain why* some delegates from other states opposed this plan.

- **Hints**: You must present reasons or causes that explain *why* the event occurred. Here you want to explain *why* some delegates opposed the plan presented by the larger states.

- **Model Answer**:

The larger states hoped they could use their size to control the new national government. Smaller states feared that if they were only represented in the new national government in proportion to their size, their interests would be ignored by the larger states. For this reason, the delegates from the smaller states opposed this proposal.

Notice how the model answer explains the main reason why the delegates from the smaller states opposed the plan presented by the larger states: they did not want to be ignored by the new national government.

Now that you have studied the "action words," examine the following example of a constructed-response question.

A SAMPLE QUESTION

Directions: You should take about 5 minutes to read the following notice and use it with what you already know to complete this task.

— NOTICE —

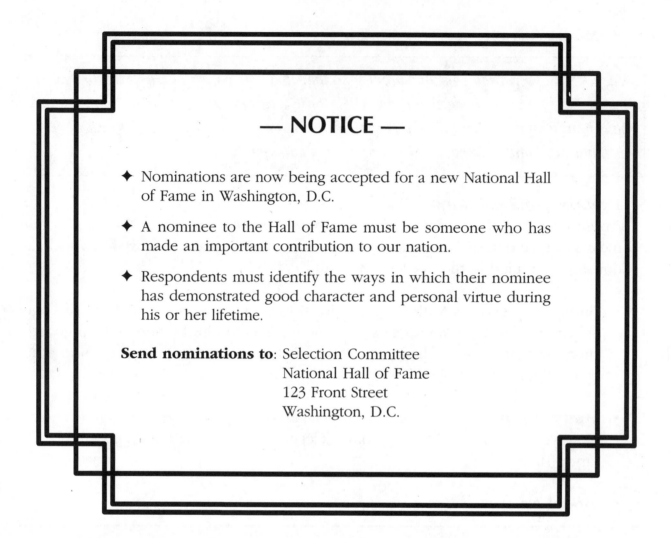

- ✦ Nominations are now being accepted for a new National Hall of Fame in Washington, D.C.
- ✦ A nominee to the Hall of Fame must be someone who has made an important contribution to our nation.
- ✦ Respondents must identify the ways in which their nominee has demonstrated good character and personal virtue during his or her lifetime.

Send nominations to: Selection Committee
National Hall of Fame
123 Front Street
Washington, D.C.

On the lines provided, *identify* your nominee to the National Hall of Fame and *explain* the reasons for your choice

Selection Committee
National Hall of Fame
123 Front Street
Washington, D.C.

Dear Committee Members:

I would like to enter the name of ____________________

as someone who deserves to be included in our National Hall of Fame. I would like to explain one reason why my nominee is a good choice. ____________

____

____

____

____

____

____

____

____

____

Sincerely,

____
(Sign your name)

The benchmark being tested in this question asks you to "identify and explain how individuals in history demonstrated good character and personal virtue" [I.2.MS.4].

A MODEL ANSWER

The following represents a model answer.

Selection Committee
National Hall of Fame
123 Front Street
Washington, D.C.

Dear Committee Members:

I would like to enter the name of Mercy Otis Warren as someone who deserves to be included in our National Hall of Fame. I would like to explain the reasons for nominating this person. Mercy Otis Warren lived in colonial times. She helped to set up the first association of colonists who opposed British policies. Later, she wrote plays and pamphlets that made fun of the British. She did this at a time when her actions put her in danger of being punished by the British. In 1808, she wrote a three-volume history of the American Revolution. Her activities helped lead the colonists to independence at a time when it was difficult for women to be active in politics.

For these reasons, I think Mercy Otis Warren showed good character and personal virtue. She deserves a place of honor in our National Hall of Fame.

Sincerely,

____

(Your name)

← Here you identify the name of your nominee

← Here you explain the reasons for your choice

← Here you link your nominee to the focus of the question

CHAPTER 6

GEOGRAPHY

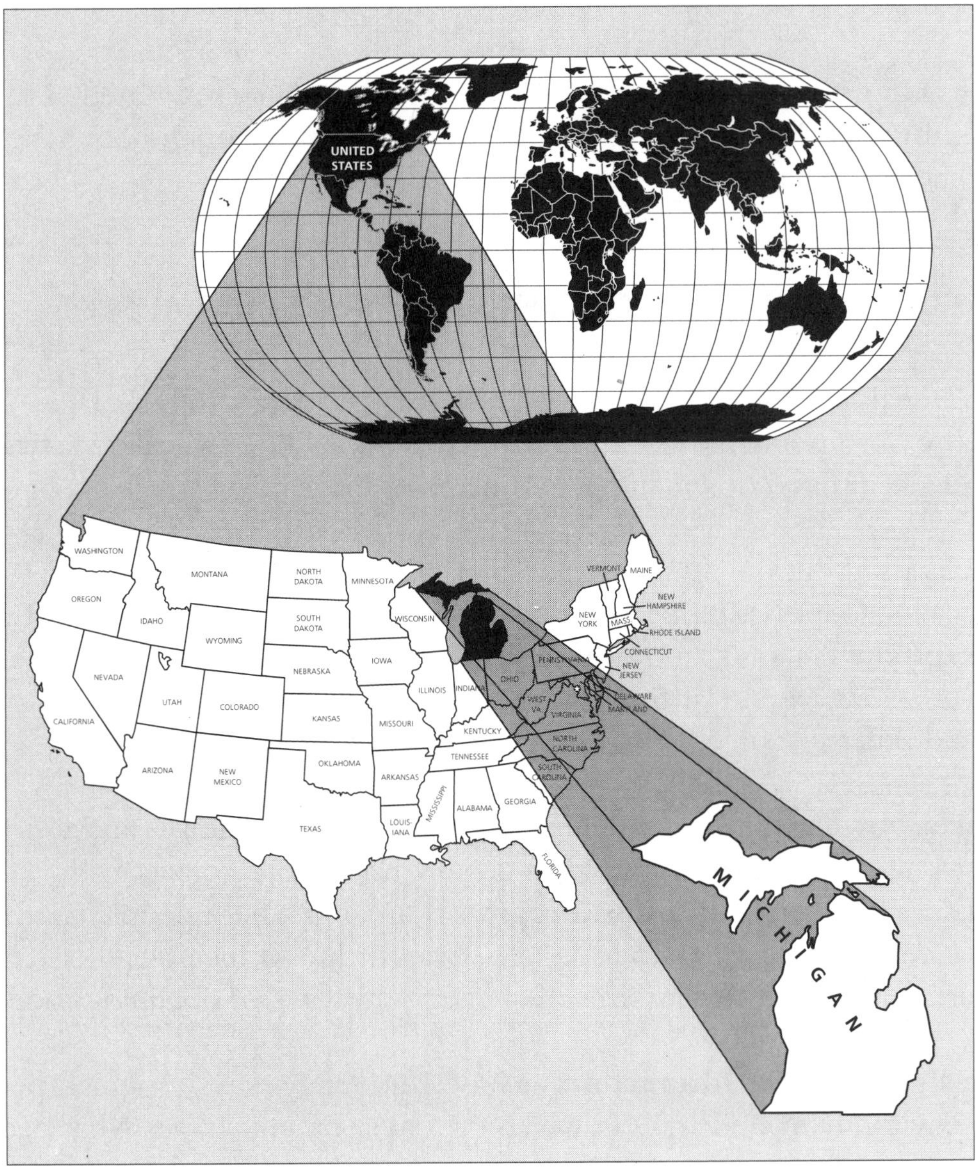

SECTION 1: A Capsule Summary of Geography

SECTION 2: Major Geographic Terms and Concepts

SECTION 3: The "Big Ideas" in Geography

SECTION 4: Practice Questions

SECTION 1 A CAPSULE SUMMARY OF GEOGRAPHY

Geography is the study of the Earth's surface, where things are located, and how they are affected by their location and physical environment. Geographers have identified five major themes in the study of geography:

THE FIVE MAJOR THEMES OF GEOGRAPHY

Location deals with where a place is located in relation to other places. To help us find any fixed point on the Earth, mapmakers draw lines — called **latitude** and **longitude** — up and down and across maps of the Earth.

Place tells us about the special features of a location that make it different from other locations. Special terms are used to describe the characteristics of a place. **Topography** refers to its land surface features. **Climate** means its weather conditions over a long period of time. **Natural resources** are its minerals, soil, fresh water, and other resources found in nature.

Regions are areas with common characteristics, such as climate and topography. People within a **geographical region** usually have more contact with each other than outside the region. A **cultural region** is an area where people share a common culture. **Culture** refers to a people's way of life. It includes their language, music, art, religion, clothing, forms of shelter, and ways of obtaining food.

Human-Environment Interaction includes the many ways in which people affect the environment, and ways in which the environment shapes what people do.

Movement refers to the movement of goods, services, ideas, and people from one place to another.

To do well on the Social Studies MEAP Test for grade 8, you must know about major world regions and cultures. Let's survey some of these regions and cultures.

NORTH AMERICA

North America is the world's third largest continent. It is bordered by three oceans: the Atlantic, Pacific, and Arctic. South of Mexico, the land changes to a narrow strip known as Central America, which is connected to South America.

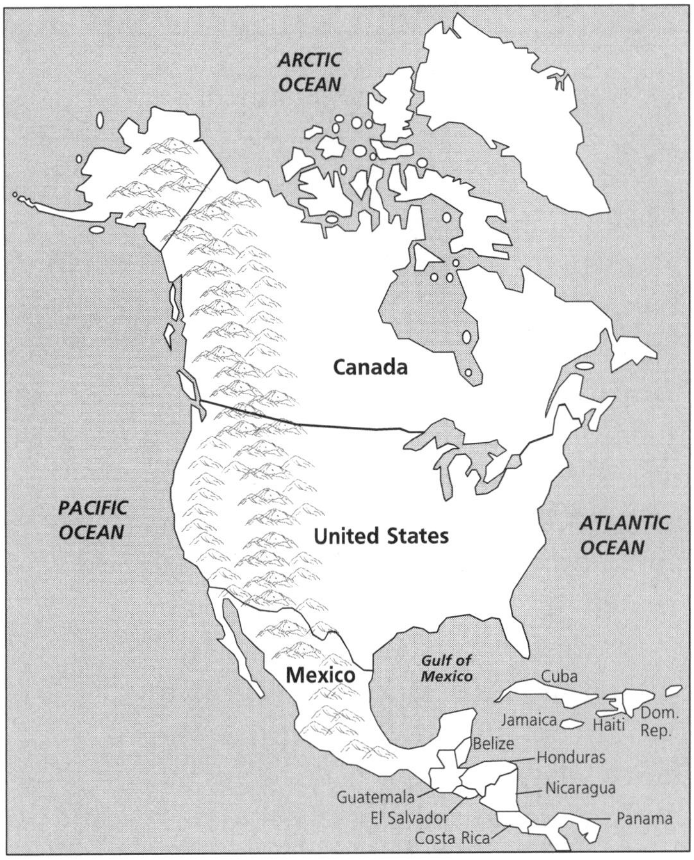

The Impact of Geography

For much of its history, North America's location separated it from the civilizations of Africa, Asia, and Europe.

North America has a wide range of climates. In the north, it is extremely cold in winter, while in the south, the climate is generally hot. In Mexico, most people live on a high plateau in the center of the country because the climate is cooler there. North America's major mountain ranges extend along its western side, from Canada down to Mexico. To the east of these mountain ranges are plains with fertile farmland.

Because of Central America's proximity to North America, the United States exercised special influence over this region in the 19th century. The United States built a canal through Panama to connect the Atlantic and Pacific Oceans.

Cultures of North America

North America was first inhabited by people descended from Asian hunters. They migrated across a land bridge connecting Siberia and Alaska thousands of years ago. Later, waves of European colonists and immigrants arrived. The French colonized the area of Quebec, while the British occupied the Atlantic seaboard from Massachusetts to Georgia. Mexico was occupied by Spain. The colonial legacy is still felt today in the primary languages spoken in these areas. Mexicans speak Spanish, people in Quebec speak French, and most Americans and Canadians speak English.

North America is generally advanced — its people enjoy a high level of education and a high income per capita. The majority of people are Christian. Most people in Mexico and Quebec are Catholic. Most Canadians and Americans live in **nuclear families**, consisting of a mother and father and their children. The population is also largely **urban** — living in cities.

Central America consists mainly of rain forests. One of the earliest Native American civilizations, the Maya, arose there. Northeast of Central America is the **West Indies**, a large number of islands including Cuba and Jamaica. When they were European colonies, these islands produced most of the world's sugar.

SOUTH AMERICA

South America is a large continent surrounded by the Pacific and Atlantic Oceans.

> **Note:** The name "Latin America" is often applied to the Americas south of the United States: Mexico, Central America, the West Indies (*Caribbean*), and South America. This region is known as **Latin America** because the people mainly speak Spanish and Portuguese, languages both derived from Latin.

The Impact of Geography

Much of South America is warm because it is near the **equator**. The most important river is the **Amazon**, the second longest river in the world. The Amazon rain forest occupies most of northeastern South America. Mountains, rain forests, and poor soils make much of South America's land unproductive. Two exceptions are the **pampas** and **llanos,** large grassy plains in the southeast and northeast.

The **Andes Mountains** run more than 4,500 miles along western South America, and are among the highest in the world. They once were home to the great Inca empire. In more recent times, the Andes separated people in different parts of South America from one another.

Cultures of South America

Spain colonized most of South America, except for Brazil, which was once a colony of Portugal. The colonists brought the Roman Catholic religion to the area, and most South Americans are still Catholic. They speak Spanish, except for Brazilians, who speak Portuguese. Most South Americans are descended from Native American groups, although many can trace their ancestors back to European colonists or enslaved Africans.

AFRICA

Africa is the second largest continent in area, and is almost three times the size of the United States. Today, this continent contains more than 50 countries. Geographers often divide Africa into two separate regions: North Africa and sub-Saharan Africa.

- **North Africa**, whose people are mainly Muslims of Arab descent, is often considered to be more closely tied to the Middle East than to the rest of Africa.

- **Sub-Saharan Africa** *(the area south of the Sahara Desert)* with its non-Arab populations, it is often considered a separate and distinct region.

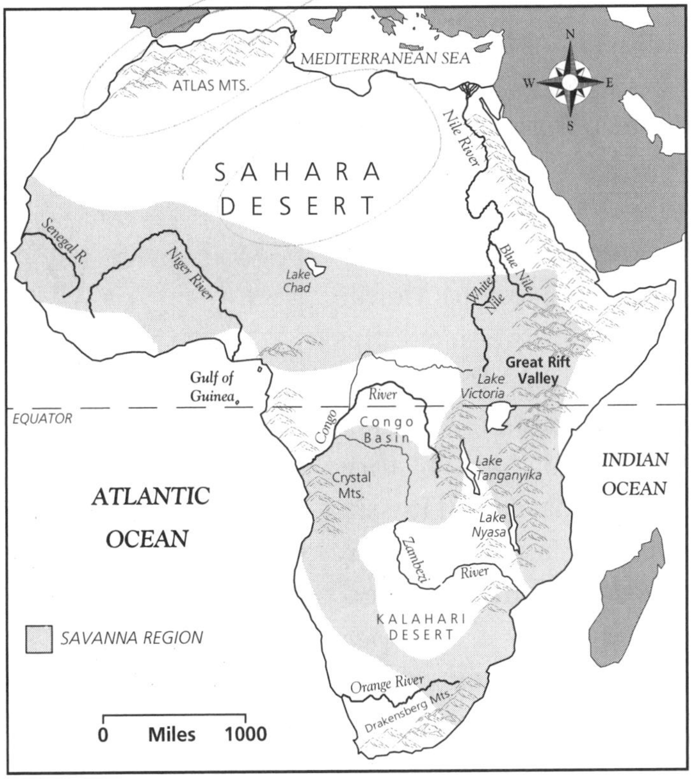

The Impact of Geography

The **Sahara**, the world's largest desert, takes up much of North Africa. For centuries it has been a barrier separating the peoples north and south of it.

A large part of sub-Saharan Africa is **savanna** *(land where wild grasses grow)*, excellent for growing crops and raising livestock. Mountains and deserts kept different groups apart, and they developed separate cultures, languages, and traditions. Most of Africa has hot summers and mild winters. The southern edge of West Africa and much of Central Africa is **tropical rain forest**, with 60 to 100 inches of rainfall a year.

Cultures of Africa

Africans are a mixture of races. The vast majority living south of the Sahara are blacks. There are also people of European and Asian descent who consider themselves Africans. The basic unit of traditional African society is the **extended family**, consisting of several generations. Related families often live together in the same village. Groups of villages with the same language and customs form a tribe. However, some tribes are **nomadic** *(wandering)* herdsmen. Africans are divided among Muslims, Christians, and followers of traditional religions.

From the 700s to the 1500s, some African tribes developed sophisticated kingdoms of considerable wealth. In the late 1800s, most of Africa was colonized by Europeans, who introduced Christianity, new ideas and advanced technologies. After World War II, Africans freed themselves from colonial rule. Since independence, significant changes in African lifestyles have taken place. There has been an expansion of education, a growth in industries, and the movement of people from the countryside to the cities.

EUROPE

Europe and Asia share the same huge land mass, which geographers divide into two continents. The dividing line runs through the center of Russia, along the Ural Mountains to the Caspian Sea and southwest to the Black Sea. On its other sides, Europe is surrounded by water — the Baltic Sea, Arctic Ocean and North Sea to the north, the Atlantic Ocean to the west, and the Mediterranean and Black Sea to the south.

The Impact of Geography

Europe's location near Africa and the Middle East led Europeans to borrow from the cultures of those regions. Mountain ranges such as the Pyrenees and Alps separated some European peoples, who developed different languages and cultures.

Much of Europe consists of a broad, fertile plain. To the east, this flat plain has few defensible frontiers. Thus, throughout its history, the borders of Russia, Poland, and Germany have constantly shifted. Because of Europe's dense population, different ethnic groups live close to one another. As a result, Europe has had many wars.

Cultures of Europe

Much of Europe was united in ancient times by the Roman empire. After the empire's collapse, various tribes migrated to different parts of Europe. Eventually they developed separate kingdoms and cultures, such as England, Spain, France, and Germany. These kingdoms were frequently at war and influenced each other greatly.

In the 1400s, Europeans experienced many technological advances. This led them to explore and conquer the Americas. Later, Europeans began the Industrial Revolution and colonized much of the world. After World War II, Europeans gave up their colonies but remained prosperous, with advanced economies and well-educated populations. Europeans have a rich cultural heritage spanning thousands of years. They developed democracy, philosophy, modern science, and many other key fields. The dominant religion in Europe is Christianity. However, there is great religious diversity. Christians are divided between Protestants and Catholics, and other Europeans are Jewish or Muslim.

ASIA

Asia is the world's largest continent. Today, it is home to more than two-thirds of the world's population. Because of its immense size and diversity of cultures, geographers usually think of Asia as consisting of several distinct regions.

THE MIDDLE EAST

Located in southwest Asia, the Middle East is the "crossroads of three continents." It connects Africa, Asia, and Europe. Some geographers consider North Africa as part of the Middle East.

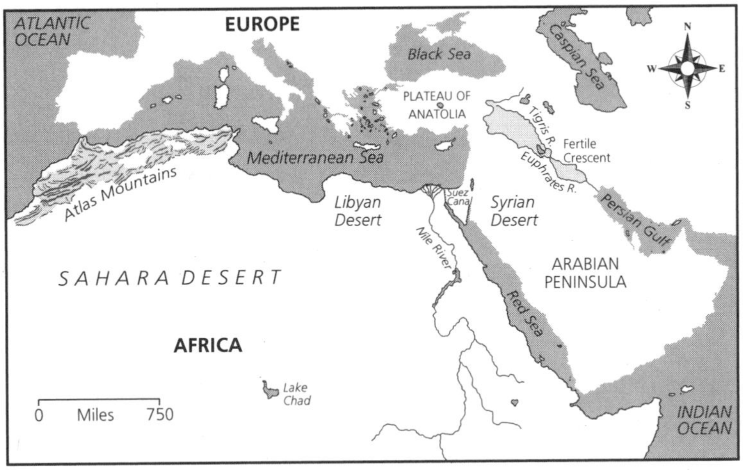

The Impact of Geography

Much of this region is desert, and the climate is very hot. As a result, most of the people live along the coasts and on major rivers, where water is plentiful and crops can be grown. In ancient times, the land in these river valleys was extremely fertile. The three major rivers in the area *(including North Africa)* are the **Nile** (*the world's longest river*), the **Tigris,** and the **Euphrates.** The Middle East provides half of the world's oil.

NORTHERN AND CENTRAL ASIA

Northern Asia is occupied by Russia, which stretches from Eastern Europe all the way east to the Pacific Ocean. Although three-quarters of Russia's population, farmland and industry are in Europe, most of its land is in Asia. Siberia, in northeastern Russia, is a cold region with forests, oil and gas deposits, gold, and diamonds. **Central Asia** is a vast corridor south of Russia and north of Iran, India and China. It is mainly an area of deserts and treeless grasslands known as **steppes**.

The Impact of Geography

Most of Russia has long, cold winters and short, mild summers. The northernmost part of Russia is **tundra** *(ground that is frozen much of the year)*. The Arctic Ocean, north of Russia, is frozen almost year-round. To the south, Russia is landlocked *(access to the sea is blocked by other countries)*. The need for a warm-water port has been a major factor in Russian history, causing its rulers to expand south and west. Because of Russia's great distance from Western Europe, its culture developed separately. It was greatly influenced by the Byzantine empire and the Mongol conquest.

Central Asia has long been a crossroads for overland trade routes between China, India, the Middle East, and Europe. Because the steppes of Central Asia provided excellent grazing land, its people were cattle herders and excellent horsemen. Throughout much of history, warriors on horseback from the Central Asian steppes periodically emerged to conquer people in neighboring lands.

EAST ASIA

East Asia includes three important countries: (1) China, (2) Korea, and (3) Japan.

China is the world's third largest country in area: only Russia and Canada are larger. For most of its history, China has been the world's most populated nation. **Korea** is a peninsula that extends from the northeast coast of China.

The Impact of Geography

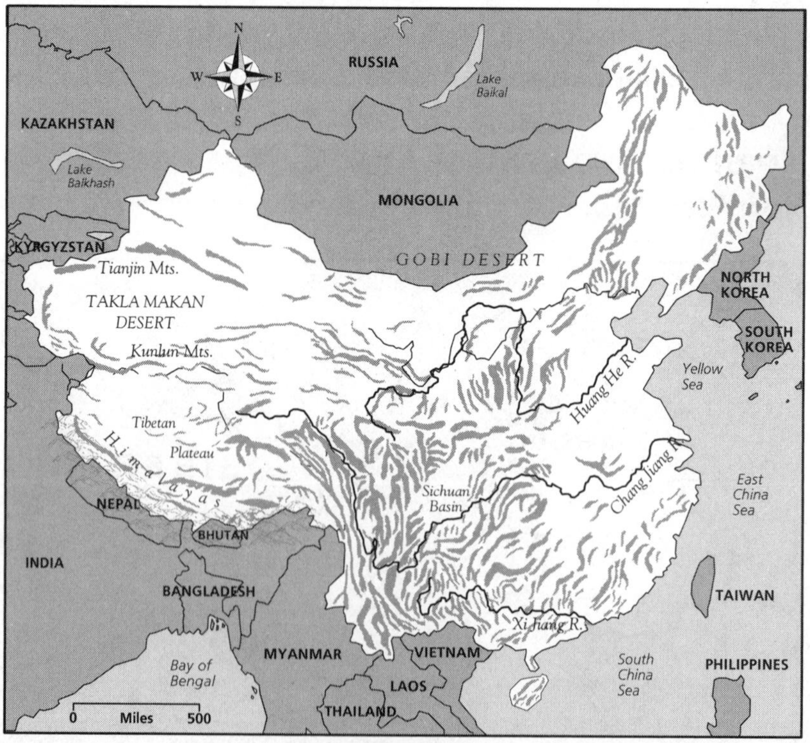

China's southern and western borders are ringed by some of the world's highest, most rugged mountains — the Himalaya, Kunlun, and Tianjin Mountains — which often protected and isolated China from the outside world. The **Gobi Desert** to the north and the Pacific Ocean to the east have further isolated China.

Eastern China consists of a vast plain with fertile river valleys. As a result, most of China's population settled in this area.

The mountains, deserts, and seas surrounding China permitted it to develop a uniform culture in isolation from other world centers of civilization. This encouraged a centralization of power and a concentration of resources that made China one of the most advanced civilizations for thousands of years.

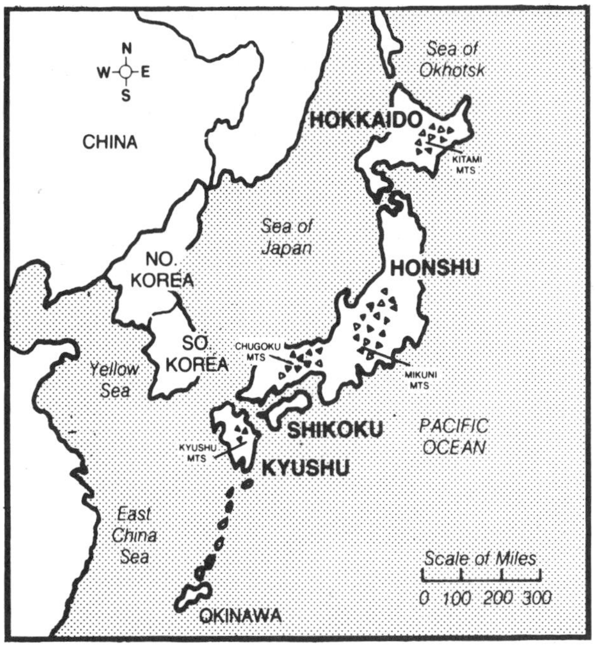

Japan lies east of the Asian mainland, separated from Korea and Russia by the Sea of Japan. Japan consists of four main islands and thousands of smaller ones, extending 1,500 miles from its northern tip to its southern end.

The Impact of Geography

Japan is a small country, and 85% of its land is covered by mountains. Nevertheless, Japan is quite densely populated. This has led to a social closeness and promoted the ability of its people to work together. Japan lacks many important natural resources necessary for its modern industries, and must import what it needs. In modern times, Japan's scarce natural resources have caused it to seek raw materials from other nations, either through trade or military conquest.

South Asia

South Asia consists of a **subcontinent** (*a large land mass that is smaller than a continent*). This subcontinent forms a triangle about half the size of the United States, jutting into the Indian Ocean. It contains India, Pakistan, Bangladesh, and several smaller nations.

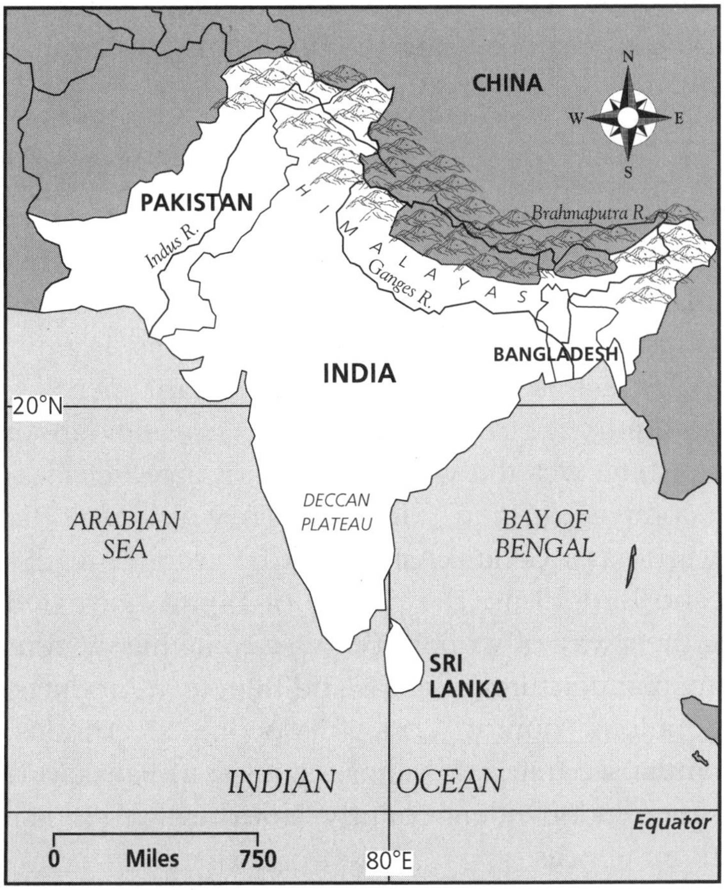

The Impact of Geography

The **Himalaya Mountains** are the highest in the world and separate the Indian subcontinent from the rest of Asia. The area's main rivers, the **Indus** and **Ganges**, were the sites of some of the world's earliest civilizations. The subcontinent's nearness to the Middle East later led to the spread of Islam throughout much of South Asia.

SOUTHEAST ASIA

Southeast Asia consists of a large peninsula on the southeast corner of the Asian mainland and the islands south and east of this peninsula. The major countries of Southeast Asia are Myanmar *(Burma)*, Thailand, Vietnam, Loas, Cambodia *(Kampuchea)*, Indonesia, Malaysia, and the Philippines. The Mekong, Salween, and Irrawaddy Rivers run through Southeast Asia.

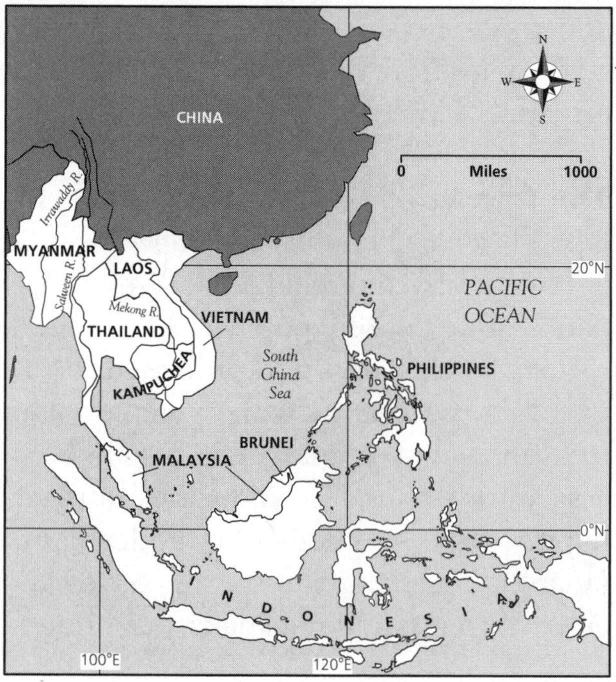

The Impact of Geography

Southeast Asia provides the shortest route between the Pacific and Indian Oceans. As a result, the region has been strongly influenced by the Chinese, Indians, Arabs, and European colonial powers. The islands of Southeast Asia export spices such as pepper and cinnamon, used in cooking worldwide. In earlier times, these spices were highly prized in Europe and the Mideast because they provided a way of preserving food that was more flavorful than using only salt. The most important climatic feature of Southeast Asia are the **monsoons**, winds that bring heavy summer rains. Rain helps to water the crops and to support life. However, if the monsoons bring too much rain, they cause flooding, property damage, and death.

CULTURES OF ASIA

Each of the principal regions of Asia has its own cultural heritage. The **Middle East**, in Southwest Asia, was the birthplace of Western civilization and of three great **monotheistic** *(belief in one God)* religions — Judaism, Christianity, and Islam. Today, the Middle East is populated by Arab and non-Arab peoples, most of whom are Muslims. Islam is also widespread in Central Asia, much of which is still populated by nomadic herders.

China, the world's most populous country, began in the Huang He valley about 6,000 years ago. For most of its history, China was the world's most advanced civilization. The Chinese invented paper, the compass, printing, and silk. They also built the Great Wall to protect China from the warriors of Central Asia. The Chinese follow philosophies like Taoism, Confucianism, and Buddhism. The people of **Japan** borrowed greatly from Chinese culture, including their way of writing. Because of its highly educated work force, Japan is now a leading manufacturer of autos and high-tech products.

India is the world's second most populous country. Most of its people are Hindus. In 1947, Hindus and Muslims living in India separated. Muslims migrated to Pakistan, a part of British India that became a separate independent country. **Southeast Asia** has Indian, Chinese, Muslim, and European influences.

SECTION 2

MAJOR GEOGRAPHIC TERMS AND CONCEPTS

Terms and concepts are important to the study of geography. Use the following graphic organizer to see how many you can recall.

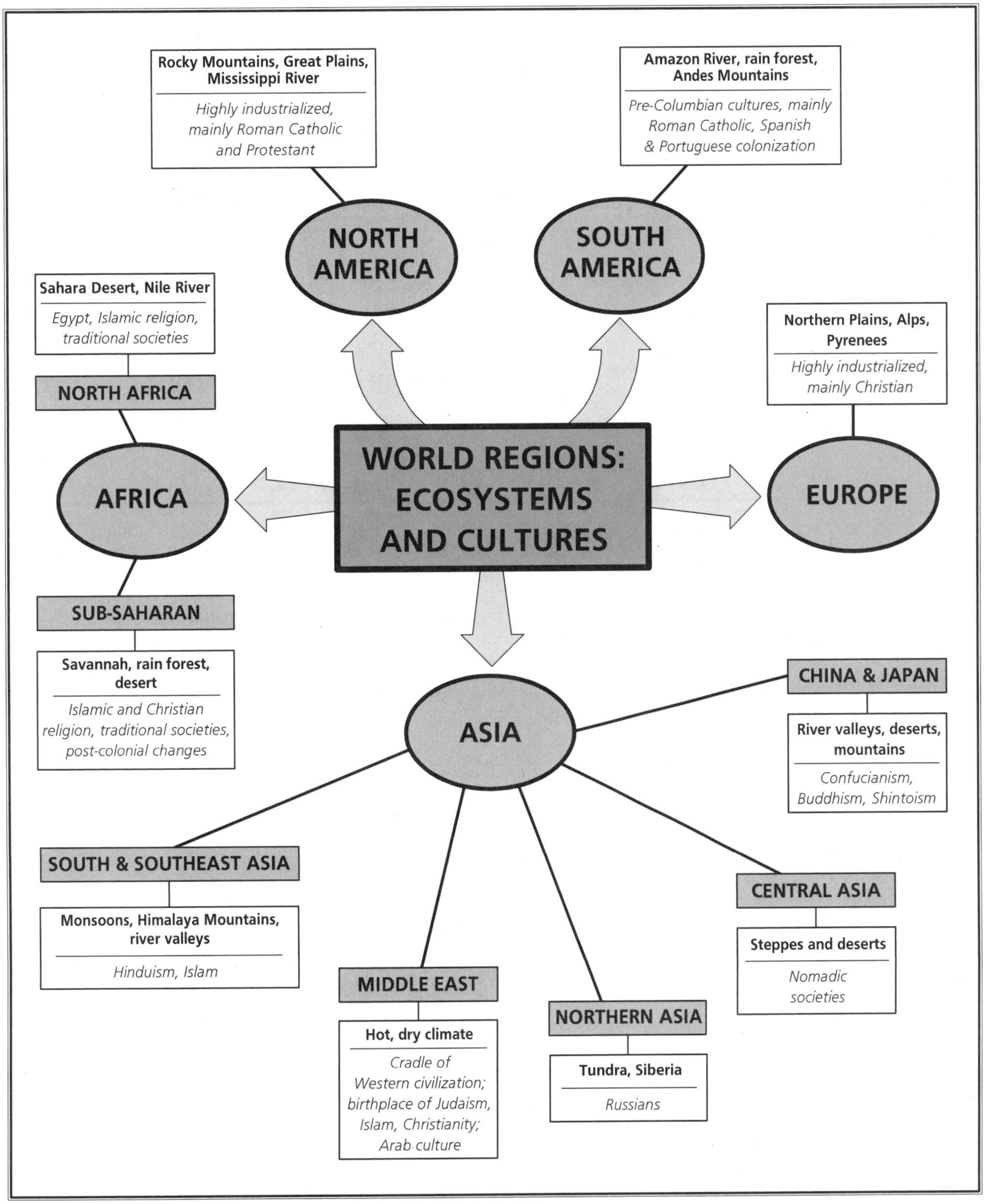

SECTION 3

THE "BIG IDEAS" IN GEOGRAPHY

In Chapter 5, you learned that it is not possible to answer MEAP Test questions correctly simply by understanding the prompt. Prompts are used to test your knowledge of the "big ideas" in social studies. It is important for you to understand the "big ideas" that will be included on the test. This section identifies the "big ideas" for geography, grouped by standard.

STANDARD II.1: DIVERSITY OF PEOPLE, PLACES, AND CULTURES

This standard focuses on the characteristics of different human cultures around the world. You should know the locations of major world cultures and be able to describe and compare their characteristics, including language, religion, beliefs, gender roles, and traditions. You should also be able to explain why people live and work as they do in different regions of the world.

STANDARD II.2: HUMAN / ENVIRONMENT INTERACTION

This standard looks at interactions between people and their physical environment. You should be able to locate, describe, and compare major world ecosystems — such as the Amazon rain forest, Andes Mountains, Sahara Desert, African savanna, Central Asian steppes, and the North European Plain. You should also be able to explain the forces that created these ecosystems. Finally, you should be able to explain the importance of these ecosystems to human life, how humans sometimes modify the environment, and how humans interact with various types of environments. For example, why did humans cut down the forests of Northern Europe and what were the effects of their actions? What have been the effects of the more recent harvesting of timber in the Amazon rain forest?

Destruction in the Amazon Rain Forest today

STANDARD II.3: LOCATION, MOVEMENT, AND CONNECTIONS

This standard examines world economic activities and global interdependence. You should be able to locate and describe major economic activities and occupations in major regions and explain why these activities are located where they are. For example, Japan is a center for manufacturing. You should also be able to explain how the world is divided into different countries, and how people, goods, services, and information move between them. Your examination of global economic interdependence should include an exploration of the political and economic connections between the United States and different world regions. For example, you should be familiar with the trade of goods and services between the United States, Canada, and Mexico under the North American Trade Agreement (NAFTA).

STANDARD II.4: REGIONS, PATTERNS, AND PROCESSES

This standard focuses on the regional concept — especially the main physical characteristics of the world's major regions, and their impact on human population and patterns of human culture. You should be able to divide the world into regions and identify the major physical and cultural characteristics of each region. You should also be able to draw a simple map of the world from memory. Your map should show the location of the seven continents, four oceans, and major seas, rivers, mountain ranges, deserts, countries, and cities. You should also be able to describe some of the geological and natural processes that created those physical features. Finally, you should be able to identify major patterns of population distribution and human culture and be able to explain the factors behind those patterns.

STANDARD II.5: GLOBAL ISSUES AND EVENTS

This standard requires you to stay informed about current events and to understand their connections to world geography. You should be able to describe events taking place in various world regions — such as how disputes between nations may be for control over regional resources. You should know how changes in the world can have global consequences. For example, the development of the internal combustion engine for automobiles has led to the pollution of the atmosphere and global warming. Lastly, you should be able to explain how geographical factors often influence the course of events. For example, Israel's small size and location — surrounded by Arab states — help explain some of the difficulties in resolving current problems between Israel and its neighbors in the Middle East.

SECTION 4

PRACTICE QUESTIONS

This section starts with two clusters of practice selected-response questions. This section also contains two constructed-response questions. Each one has a prompt and a writing task related to it. Examine each prompt carefully and write your answers as directed. Each question has a benchmark number to indicate which "big idea" is being tested. A list of the geography benchmarks is at the end of this chapter.

— SELECTED-RESPONSE QUESTIONS —

Directions: Read the passage below and use it with what you already know to answer the questions that follow.

MAJOR WORLD RELIGIONS

Listed below is a short description of five of the world's major religions.

Religion A. Followers of this religion were the first people known to have believed in a single God. They believe God made a promise to protect them, so long as they obeyed the Ten Commandments — a set of rules by which to live. Members of this religion believe that God expects them to act justly towards others.

Religion B. Followers of this religion also believe in one God. They take their name from Jesus Christ of Nazareth, who spoke of forgiveness, selflessness, and repentance. They believe Jesus was the son of God who sacrificed himself for the sins of humanity.

Religion C. Followers of this religion also believe in one all-powerful God known as Allah. They believe Allah has complete control over each person's actions. They base their religious beliefs on the teachings of Mohammed. Believers try to visit the city of Mecca at least once in their lifetime, and must give charity to the poor.

Religion D. Followers of this religion worship many gods and goddesses. They believe at death, a person's spirit leaves the body to be reborn in another living thing. If a person behaved well in his or her lifetime, that person would be rewarded by having a better life when he or she was reborn. Followers of this religion are forbidden to eat beef.

Religion E. This religion is based on the teachings of Siddhartha Gautama, an Indian prince who searched for the true meaning of life. Siddhartha taught that excessive desires are the main causes of pain and suffering. Instead of seeking wealth, he believed a person should try to discover the true meaning of life.

1 Which religion is most popular in the Middle East and North Africa?

A Religion A
B Religion B
C Religion C
D Religion D

II.1.MS.2

2 In which country did TWO of the religions discussed in the passage begin?

A Great Britain
B China
C India
D Brazil

II.1.MS.1

3 Which conclusion BEST applies to all five religions?

A All five religions provide guidance for living a moral life.
B Most of their followers believe Jesus was the son of God.
C All five religions oppose acquiring personal wealth and property.
D All their members worship only one God.

II.1.MS.3

4 Which region of the world was the birthplace to THREE of the religions discussed in the reading passage?

A Africa
B Middle East
C Latin America
D Europe

II.4.MS.4

5 Which was a result of the conflict between followers of Religions C and D?

A The separate countries of India and Pakistan were created.
B A civil war began between Irish Catholics and British Protestants.
C The former Soviet Union banned religious worship.
D Both religions merged into a unified system of beliefs.

II.5.MS.1

Name ______________________ Teacher ______________________

Directions: Read the following passage and use it with what you already know to answer the questions that follow.

GLOBAL ECOSYSTEMS

The world's ecosystems vary considerably in size, climate, and composition.

Ecosystem 1. This ecosystem has a tropical climate. Most of the land is covered with grass, scattered flat-topped trees, and bushes. During the rainy season, the grasses grow quite tall. During the winter dry season, the area is still warm but gets little or no rainfall. The grasses and shrubs support many species of birds and mammals not found elsewhere. The area is not densely populated by humans.

Ecosystem 2. This ecosystem exists in hot and humid areas where rainfall is extremely heavy — from 60 to 120 inches per year. Plant life consists of huge trees, growing so close together their tops shade the ground, preventing undergrowth from developing in many areas. Many unique plant and animal species live here.

Ecosystem 3. The vast area of this ecosystem, larger than the continental United States, covers more than a third of Africa. It is a region of windswept rock, gravel, and shifting sand dunes. In parts of this ecosystem, daytime temperatures can reach 130° F. Ten years can pass without rainfall.

Ecosystem 4. This ecosystem is found in the lands south of the Arctic and north of great forests. It is characterized by low hills and marshy plains covered with snow and ice for most of the year. The ground is almost always frozen. The main vegetation consists of moss, small shrubs, and low grasses.

Ecosystem 5. This ecosystem exists in a region of vast rolling plains and low hills. Its rich, fertile soils, considered among the best in the world, make it ideal for farming. Summers are hot and winters are cold. Once heavily forested, the land has been cleared. Today, this ecosystem is marked by large human populations, with large cities and busy factories.

6 Caravans of camels carrying goods would MOST likely be seen in which ecosystem?

A Ecosystem 1 **C** Ecosystem 3
B Ecosystem 2 **D** Ecosystem 4

II.2.MS.2

7 In which TWO countries would you expect to find Ecosystem 2 located?

A The United States and Saudi Arabia
B Brazil and Indonesia
C France and Egypt
D Israel and Canada

II.2.MS.1

8 In which ecosystem would you expect to find the GREATEST population density?

A Ecosystem 2 **C** Ecosystem 4
B Ecosystem 3 **D** Ecosystem 5

II.2.MS.3

9 Which occupations would you expect to be most common in Ecosystem 4?

A farming, beach lifeguards, and factory workers
B computer engineers, industrialists, and farmers
C fishing, hunting, and herding
D florists, fishing, and farming

II.3.MS.2

10 What geographic term would MOST accurately describe the features found in Ecosystem 1?

A rain forest **C** desert
B jungle **D** tundra

II.2.MS.2

Name ______________________ Teacher ______________________

— CONSTRUCTED-RESPONSE QUESTIONS —

Following are two constructed-response questions. Read the directions and examine each question carefully before answering. Each question has a benchmark number to show you which "big idea" is being tested.

Directions: You should take about 5 minutes to read the following passage and use it with what you already know to complete this task.

Technology and scientific advances often bring positive changes to humankind. For example, the development of the internal combustion engine is often viewed as one of the greatest advances of all time. This achievement led not only to the development of automobiles, but also tanks, trucks, and airplanes. These made it possible to travel, to communicate, and to produce and distribute goods more effectively. But these positive developments were also accompanied by some disadvantages.

11 On the lines provided, identify **one** harmful consequence of the scientific advance mentioned in the passage. Explain how this consequence was harmful.

Identification of one harmful consequence: ______________________________

____

Explanation of how it was harmful: ______________________________

____

____

____

____

____

II.5.MS.1

Name ______________________ Teacher ______________________

Directions: You should take about 5 minutes to read the following passage and use it with what you already know to complete this task.

It is important to have a clear picture of the world we live in. Geographers have divided our world into areas called regions. In the blank space below, sketch from memory a map of one region of the world. Then label the region, one of its key physical features, and any oceans that border it.

II.4.MS.1

Name ______________________________ Teacher ______________________________

BENCHMARKS OF THE GEOGRAPHY STRAND

Standard II.1: Diversity of People, Places, and Cultures

II.1.MS.1 Locate and describe the diverse places, cultures, and communities of major world regions.

II.1.MS.2 Describe and compare characteristics of major world cultures including language, religion, belief systems, gender roles, and traditions.

II.1.MS.3 Explain why people live and work as they do in different regions.

Standard II.2: Human/Environment Interaction

II.2.MS.1 Locate, describe, and compare the ecosystems, resources, and human-environment interactions of major world regions.

II.2.MS.2 Locate major ecosystems, describe their characteristics, and explain the process that created them.

II.2.MS.3 Explain the importance of different kinds of ecosystems to people.

II.2.MS.4 Explain how humans modify the environment and describe some of the possible consequences of those modifications.

II.2.MS.5 Describe the consequences of human/environment interactions in several different types of environments.

Standard II.3: Location, Movement, and Connections

II.3.MS.1 Locate and describe major economic activities and occupations of major world regions and explain the reasons for their locations.

II.3.MS.2 Explain how governments have divided land and sea areas into different regions.

II.3.MS.3 Describe how and why people, goods and services, and information move within world regions and between regions.

II.3.MS.4 Describe the major economic and political connections between the United States and different world regions and explain their causes and consequences.

Standard II.4: Regions, Patterns, and Processes

II.4.MS.1 Draw sketch maps of the world from memory.

II.4.MS.2 Locate and describe major cultural, economic, political and environmental features of Africa, Europe, Asia, Australia, and North and South America and the processes that created them.

II.4.MS.3 Describe the major patterns of world population, physical features, ecosystems, cultures and explain some of the factors causing the patterns.

II.4.MS.4 Compare major world regions with respect to cultures, economy, governmental systems, environment, and communications.

Standard II.5: Global Issues and Events

II.5.MS.1 Describe how social and scientific changes in regions may have global consequences.

II.5.MS.2 Describe the geographic aspects of events taking place in different world regions.

II.5.MS.3 Explain how elements of the physical geography, culture, and history of a region may be influencing current events.

CHAPTER 7

HISTORY

British and Americans fight at Bunker Hill

George Washington in 1785

Sea battle during the War of 1812

Section 1: A Capsule Summary of History

Section 2: Major Historical Terms and Concepts

Section 3: The "Big Ideas" in History

Section 4: Practice Questions

SECTION 1 — A CAPSULE SUMMARY OF HISTORY

On the eighth grade Social Studies MEAP Test, you will mainly be responsible for knowing about the history of the United States from 1754 to 1815. The following summary will help you recall important information to prepare for the test.

THE NATURE OF HISTORY

The word "history" refers to what happened in the past. Historians attempt to understand and explain past events and ways of life. Historians depend upon two kinds of sources to learn about the past:

- ✦ **Primary Sources**. These are original records of an event or way of life that is under investigation. Primary sources include eyewitness reports, official records from the time of the event, letters sent by people involved in the event, diaries, and photographs. All historical information used to reconstruct past events can be traced back to primary sources.

- ✦ **Secondary Sources**. These are the writings and interpretations of historians and other writers. Secondary sources such as textbooks and articles often provide convenient summaries of the information that was originally found in primary sources.

To interpret the information contained in their sources, historians must be able to tell the difference between an opinion and a fact. An **opinion** is a statement of belief. A **fact** is a statement about something that really happened. Historians often check several sources to verify *(make sure)* that a statement of fact is correct.

THE FRENCH AND INDIAN WAR, 1754-1763

In North America, British colonists gradually established settlements along the Atlantic coast from Massachusetts to Virginia. By the 1750s, the British were claiming control of the Ohio River Valley in the west. Meanwhile, the French had established "New France" in what is now eastern Canada. The French built a string of forts along the St. Lawrence River and the Great Lakes to keep British fur traders and settlers from crossing into lands claimed by France.

Britain and France became engaged in a global contest for colonies and control of the seas. War between them finally broke out in 1754. Because many Native American tribes sided with the French, the contest in North America became known as the **French and Indian War**. A British force under General James Wolfe surprised the French at Quebec and captured the city in 1759, giving the British control of the St. Lawrence River. Three years later, France surrendered to Britain. Canada and all lands east of the Mississippi River became British territory. The end of the war promised an era of peace and prosperity for British colonists. But the defeat of France also set the stage for the American Revolution twelve years later.

THE AMERICAN REVOLUTION, 1775-1783

British leaders believed that colonies existed for the benefit of the "mother country" ruling them. American colonists were expected to sell crops like tobacco to the British at a low price. In exchange, the colonists were expected to buy more expensive British goods, such as manufactured products. British colonists in America, on the other hand, felt they no longer needed the protection of Britain once the French threat was removed. This helps explain why differences developed between the colonists and Britain.

George III, the British king

ROOTS OF THE AMERICAN REVOLUTION

To prevent further Native American attacks, the British government declared in 1763 that no colonists could settle west of the Appalachian Mountains. This so-called "Proclamation Line" was greatly resented by western settlers. The British government also proposed new taxes on the colonists to repay Britain for the cost of protecting the colonies during the French and Indian War. When these taxes were passed by the British Parliament without consulting the American colonists, the colonists protested. They particularly objected to the **Stamp Act** (1765) which taxed newspapers, books, and official documents.

Colonists protest the Stamp Act

In response to these protests, the British eventually canceled almost all of the new taxes except for the duties on tea. In 1773, the colonists protested against this tax by dumping a shipment of British tea into Boston harbor. This protest became known as the **Boston Tea Party.** It brought a sharp reaction from the British. They closed Boston Harbor and restricted the freedom of citizens in Massachusetts, greatly increasing tensions between the colonists and Great Britain.

The Idea of Independence Emerges

Representatives from the colonies met in Philadelphia to discuss their common problems. This assembly, known as the **First Continental Congress**, decided to continue the protest against British taxes. In 1775, shots were fired between British soldiers and American colonists at Concord and Lexington, in Massachusetts. The fighting quickly spread to other colonies and marked the start of the American Revolutionary War. The British sent additional troops to put down the rebellious colonists.

The battle at Lexington that marked the start of the American Revolution

A Declaration of Independence is Issued

In 1776, representatives from all 13 colonies met again in Philadelphia to discuss the possibility of independence. After much debate, the Second Continental Congress decided to declare American independence from Britain. Thomas Jefferson was placed in charge of a committee to write a "Declaration of Independence." This document, issued on July 4, 1776, explained the reasons why the colonists sought independence from Great Britain. Jefferson believed that government was a social contract, and that citizens had a right to overthrow an oppressive government. The Declaration began with words in the scroll to the right.

> *"We hold these truths to be self-evident, that all men are created equal, that they are endowed by their Creator with certain Unalienable Rights, that among these are Life, Liberty and the pursuit of Happiness. That to secure these rights, Governments are instituted among Men, deriving their just powers from the consent of the governed, That whenever any Form of Government becomes destructive of these ends, it is the right of the People to alter or abolish it, and to institute new Government ...*

The Importance of the Declaration

The Declaration of Independence laid the foundation for the United States to become the first democratic republic in modern times, and has served as an inspiration for later generations.

SIGNIFICANCE OF THE DECLARATION OF INDEPENDENCE

Laid foundation for democratic government. The Declaration said government was created by the people, and that the U.S. government's final power would be in the hands of its citizens.

Inspired equality. When the Declaration was adopted, not all Americans were treated equally. The words "all men are created equal" set a goal that the nation has been striving to achieve for over 200 years.

Influenced the Constitution. The U.S. Constitution guarantees all citizens a number of rights. Many of these rights were based on ideas set forth in the Declaration of Independence.

Impact on revolutions abroad. Ideas expressed in the Declaration were used by others who felt oppressed by government, such as in the French Revolution (1789) and later revolutions around the world.

THE STRUGGLE FOR INDEPENDENCE (1775-1783)

In the first years of the war, the colonial army barely managed to escape from one disaster after another. Under the leadership of General George Washington, the colonists eventually won key battles in New Jersey and New York. These victories helped convince France to supply military assistance to the Americans. With French help, Washington forced the British to surrender at Yorktown, Virginia in 1781. Under the terms of the **Treaty of Paris (1783)**, the British recognized American independence and surrendered to the new United States all the lands between the Mississippi River and the Atlantic coast, from the Great Lakes to Florida.

Surrender of British General Burgoyne after the Battle of Saratoga, a turning point in the war

THE ARTICLES OF CONFEDERATION: THE NATION'S FIRST GOVERNMENT

After winning independence, each of the former colonies became an independent state. The former colonists quickly realized they also needed some form of central, or national, government. At the same time, because of their experience with the British, they were afraid of creating a central government that was too powerful. In 1781, the states adopted the **Articles of Confederation.** This agreement created a very weak central government. The state governments, not the central government, held most of the power in the new nation. It was left to each state to carry out the acts of the Confederation Congress.

IMPORTANT ACCOMPLISHMENTS

The Confederation Congress signed the peace with Britain, helped keep the new nation together, and created a method for admitting new states to the nation.

With independence, the United States found itself in possession of lands north of the Ohio River and east of the Mississippi. The Confederation Congress passed the **Northwest Ordinance of 1787**, which divided this territory into smaller areas such as Michigan and Ohio. The new law set up procedures for the eventual admission of these territories as new states when their populations increased. The Northwest Ordinance also banned slavery in the Northwest Territory, while the earlier Land Ordinance of 1785 set up provisions for creating public schools in the same region.

NEW PROBLEMS

Many feared that the new government had too little power to do its job properly. For example, the central government could not tax or borrow directly. It had to request money from the states. The central government also had no army. When a small uprising of farmers — **Shays' Rebellion** — broke out in Massachusetts in 1786, there was no national army to put it down if it spread to other states. Although the state militia was able to suppress it, people began demanding a stronger national government.

A CONSTITUTIONAL CONVENTION MEETS

In 1787, fifty-five representatives from the states met in Philadelphia to revise the Articles of Confederation. The representatives quickly decided that a new national **constitution** *(a plan for government)* was needed. It was further agreed that a stronger central government was necessary. The new national government would be led by a President, would have a national legislature and a national court system. The delegates also believed that the new government should have the power to collect its own taxes and raise an army.

The room in Philadelphia's Independence Hall where the U.S. Constitution was written

However, there were some important disagreements that were eventually settled by compromise. Two of the main compromises reached at the Constitutional Convention involved representation and slavery.

MAJOR CONSTITUTIONAL COMPROMISES

ISSUE: *How should states be represented in the national legislature?*

THE GREAT COMPROMISE: The thirteen states were of many different sizes. The larger states felt they should have a greater say in the national government. The smaller states felt each state should have an equal voice. In the Great Compromise, two "houses" were created in the legislature *(Congress)*. In the **House of Representatives**, states were represented according to their population size. This allowed states with a larger population to have a greater number of representatives. In the **Senate**, each state, no matter what its size, would be represented by two Senators. To pass a law, approval by *both* houses of Congress was required.

ISSUE: *How should slaves be counted?*

THE THREE-FIFTHS COMPROMISE: Southern states wanted slaves counted as part of their population, to have more members in the House of Representatives, but not for tax purposes. Northern states wanted slaves counted for taxation, but not for representation. The states compromised by agreeing to count every 5 slaves as 3 free persons for the purposes of both taxation and representation.

THE STATES DEBATE RATIFICATION

The members of the Constitutional Convention knew that they could not adopt their new plan of government on their own authority. They decided that before the Constitution could become law, nine states would have to **ratify** *(approve)* it. Special conventions were held in each state for this purpose.

REASONS FOR REJECTION

Opponents of the Constitution feared that a strong central government would threaten individual freedom. Government leaders could build a strong army and use it to collect unpopular taxes. Critics of the Constitution pointed out that there was no Bill of Rights in the proposed Constitution to protect important liberties such as the right to a fair trial and freedom of speech.

REASONS FOR ACCEPTANCE

Those favoring the Constitution argued that a stronger central government was needed to replace the Articles of Confederation. They also argued that there was no reason to fear that leaders of the new government would use their powers against the people. The Constitution provided that power would be separated among the different **branches** *(parts)* of the central government, and further divided between the states and the central government. Therefore, no single part of the new government could become too strong.

By the end of 1788, eleven states voted to accept the Constitution. In several states, support was won by promising that a Bill of Rights would soon be added.

The signing of the Constitution in 1787: George Washington presides, with Alexander Hamilton and Benjamin Franklin seated to the left of the platform

THE PRESIDENCY OF GEORGE WASHINGTON, 1789-1797

In 1789, George Washington was inaugurated as the first President of the United States. Two of the major problems Washington faced on coming into office were the formation of an administration and the fact that the nation's treasury was empty.

WASHINGTON'S DOMESTIC POLICY

Domestic policy refers to how a President deals with problems and conditions within the United States. **Foreign policy** concerns relations with other countries.

The First Cabinet, 1789

The Constitution allowed the President to appoint people to executive departments, but did not state what these departments should be. To help carry out his many tasks, Washington appointed a Secretary of the Treasury, a Secretary of State, a Secretary of War, and an Attorney General. Besides heading their own departments, these officials began meeting together in what came to be called the **Cabinet**. Over the years, as the government assumed greater responsibilities, new Cabinet departments were created.

The first Cabinet

Raising Money

The new nation faced a large debt from fighting the American Revolutionary War. The job of solving the nation's economic problems went to **Alexander Hamilton**, the Secretary of the Treasury. Hamilton drew up a four-part program for getting the nation on a sound financial basis:

HAMILTON'S FINANCIAL PLAN

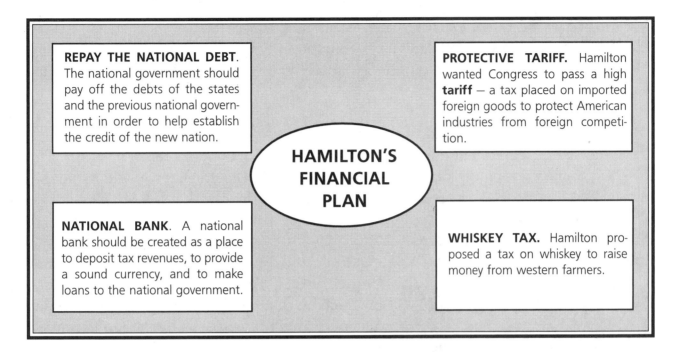

REPAY THE NATIONAL DEBT. The national government should pay off the debts of the states and the previous national government in order to help establish the credit of the new nation.

PROTECTIVE TARIFF. Hamilton wanted Congress to pass a high **tariff** — a tax placed on imported foreign goods to protect American industries from foreign competition.

NATIONAL BANK. A national bank should be created as a place to deposit tax revenues, to provide a sound currency, and to make loans to the national government.

WHISKEY TAX. Hamilton proposed a tax on whiskey to raise money from western farmers.

The Birth of Political Parties

Hamilton's financial program was strongly opposed by Thomas Jefferson, who was serving as Washington's Secretary of State. Jefferson and his followers believed that Hamilton's plan would benefit only the wealthy and hurt the majority of Americans, who were middle-income farmers. This disagreement over how government should function led Jefferson and Hamilton to organize their followers into the first American **political parties** — groups that try to elect their members to government offices so that they can pass laws favorable to their ideas. Hamilton's followers became known as the **Federalists**. Jefferson's supporters called themselves **Democratic-Republicans**.

Alexander Hamilton

Defeat of the Protective Tariff

Hamilton was not successful in his attempt to pass a protective tariff. Southern states opposed it because they felt it would benefit the industrial North and make it harder for them to sell their cash crops to Great Britain and to buy British goods.

The Whiskey Rebellion, 1794

Farmers living west of the Appalachian Mountains often converted their excess grain into whiskey. Farmers found it was cheaper to transport whiskey than bushels of grain over mountain trials. The new federal whiskey tax caused resentment among farmers.

When farmers on the Pennsylvania frontier refused to pay the tax, Washington and Hamilton called up the militia and put down the rebellion.

WASHINGTON'S FOREIGN POLICY

The new nation was weak militarily. A revolution in France led to war between France and Britain in 1793. Jefferson's supporters favored the French revolutionaries, while the Federalists favored the British.

The Proclamation of Neutrality (1793)

Many Americans feared that the United States might be drawn into the war. To prevent this, Washington adopted a policy of **neutrality** — the United States would avoid taking sides in European disputes and would not become involved in foreign wars.

Washington's Farewell Address, 1796

After two 4-year terms in office, Washington declined requests that he run a third time. He delivered a **Farewell Address** to Congress, in which he cautioned Americans against entering into permanent alliances with foreign countries. Washington wanted the nation to devote itself to developing trade and assuming leadership of the Western Hemisphere, rather than becoming involved in European conflicts.

At left: Washington bids farewell to his officers and colleagues

THE PRESIDENCY OF THOMAS JEFFERSON, 1801-1809

The next President, John Adams, was a Federalist who continued Washington's policies. In 1800, Adams lost the election to Thomas Jefferson.

Thomas Jefferson

JEFFERSON'S VIEWS ON GOVERNMENT

Jefferson viewed his election as the **Revolution of 1800**, because he believed it marked an important turning point in the direction of the nation. Jefferson believed the best government was a weak government. He opposed giving special privileges to the wealthy, and discouraged attempts to build up the nation's military power. Jefferson had strong sympathies for the common farmer. When he became President, he set about reducing the size of the army, halting plans for naval expansion, and lowering the costs of government.

The Louisiana Purchase (1803)

Jefferson had always dreamed of extending the United States westward. He soon had an opportunity to realize his dreams. The French ruler, Napoleon, offered to sell the Louisiana Territory *(which he had obtained from Spain)* to the United States for $15 million.

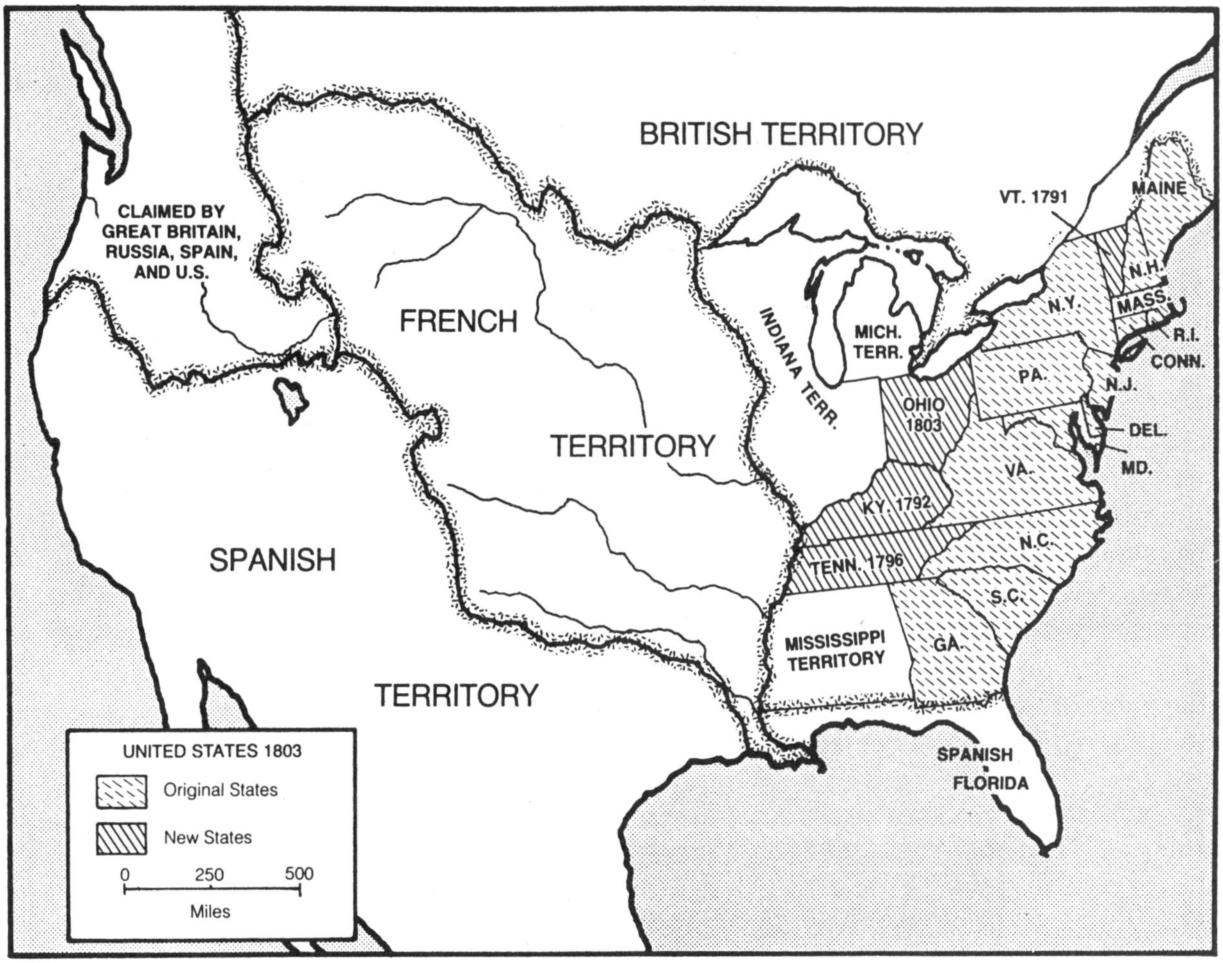

Although Jefferson was uncertain whether the Constitution allowed the national government to buy new territory, he went ahead with the purchase. The Louisiana Territory immediately doubled the size of the United States. Jefferson sent **Lewis and Clark** to explore the region. Their expedition westward to the Pacific Ocean lasted two years.

Embargo Act of 1807

With war raging between Britain and France, British warships began stopping American ships to search for deserters from the British navy. This practice humiliated Americans and put pressure on Jefferson to take action. In order to avoid war, Jefferson pushed the **Embargo Act** through Congress. American ships would no longer carry foodstuffs to France or trade with Europe. Jefferson's diplomacy succeeded in keeping the United States out of war during his Presidency, but also hurt American commerce.

THE WAR OF 1812

Only a few years after Jefferson's Presidency ended, America was drawn into conflict with Britain in the **War of 1812**. British ships had continued to stop American ships and to take American sailors. Meanwhile, some Americans, especially Westerners, thought it might be possible to conquer Canada. Soon after the war broke out, American forces tried to invade Canada, but were unsuccessful. In retaliation, British troops briefly occupied Washington, D.C. and burned down the White House. Some of the most important battles of the war were fought on the Great Lakes. In 1815, a peace treaty was signed at Ghent that left things much as they had been before the war, except that the British promised they would no longer search American ships for British deserters. One of the great heroes of the war was General Andrew Jackson, who defeated British forces at the **Battle of New Orleans** in 1815. The battle was actually fought after the war ended, because neither side yet knew that a peace treaty had already been signed.

Andrew Jackson at the Battle of New Orleans

EMERGING AMERICAN LIFESTYLES

By the early 1800s, Americans were creating their own unique culture. It was an exciting mixture of English, European, Native American, and African traditions blended together under American conditions.

Farmers

America was still a largely rural society. Crops were the foundation of the nation's wealth. Owning and working the land gave farmers freedom and independence. However, changes were on the way. New inventions and the rise of industry in the Northeast led to the growth of towns and cities.

Settlers clearing land for farming

The Rise of Industry

In the early 1800s, a new industrial society began to emerge in the Northeast. There was an increased use of machines and a shift from working at home or in small shops to working in factories. This development, known as the **Industrial Revolution**, led to new industries, expanded transportation, and rapidly growing cities. Workers in early industries often had to put in 16-hour days in crowded, poorly lit, and unsafe factories.

Women

In the early Republic, American women generally continued to follow traditional roles. They were usually excluded from public life and left in charge of the home and children. Women were denied full equality of citizenship and lacked the right to vote, serve on juries, or hold public office. In education, women were denied admission to college. Farm women had to work in the fields as well as cook, clean, make clothes, and care for their children. Working-class women often worked outside the home as servants, laundresses, cooks, and factory workers.

African Americans

Since the 1500s, enslaved Africans had been brought to the West Indies and North and South America as slaves. The invention of the cotton gin in 1793 increased the demand for African slaves in Southern plantations. However, in 1808, Congress prohibited the future importation of slaves. In the period following this law, most of the slaves in America were native-born. Generally, African Americans fell into two groups: free African Americans and slaves.

- **Free African Americans**. Many African Americans were set free following the American Revolution. Others had been freed by their owners when the owner died. Many free African Americans found jobs in a variety of occupations. However, most still faced prejudice and discrimination, even in the North. Laws kept them from voting, traveling, and serving on juries. Lastly, many free African Americans feared being kidnapped and returned to a life of slavery.

- **Slaves**. Most white Southern families had no slaves. Slaves generally were owned by wealthy Southern landholders who grew cash crops such as tobacco, cotton, and sugar. The slaves did back-breaking work on plantations as field hands. Living conditions were quite primitive. The enslaved workers ate simple, unbalanced meals of corn, pork, and molasses. However, not all slaves worked on plantations or for the wealthy. Some slaves became skilled blacksmiths or carpenters and were hired out by their owners. Even then, their wages were the property of their owners. The enslaved Africans were denied many basic human rights: for example, they could be sold apart from their families at the whim of their owners. Despite these harsh conditions, they held onto much of their African heritage and developed their own unique culture.

Enslaved workers planting tobacco seedlings

SECTION 2

MAJOR HISTORICAL TERMS AND CONCEPTS

There are many important terms and concepts in history. Use this graphic organizer to review their meanings.

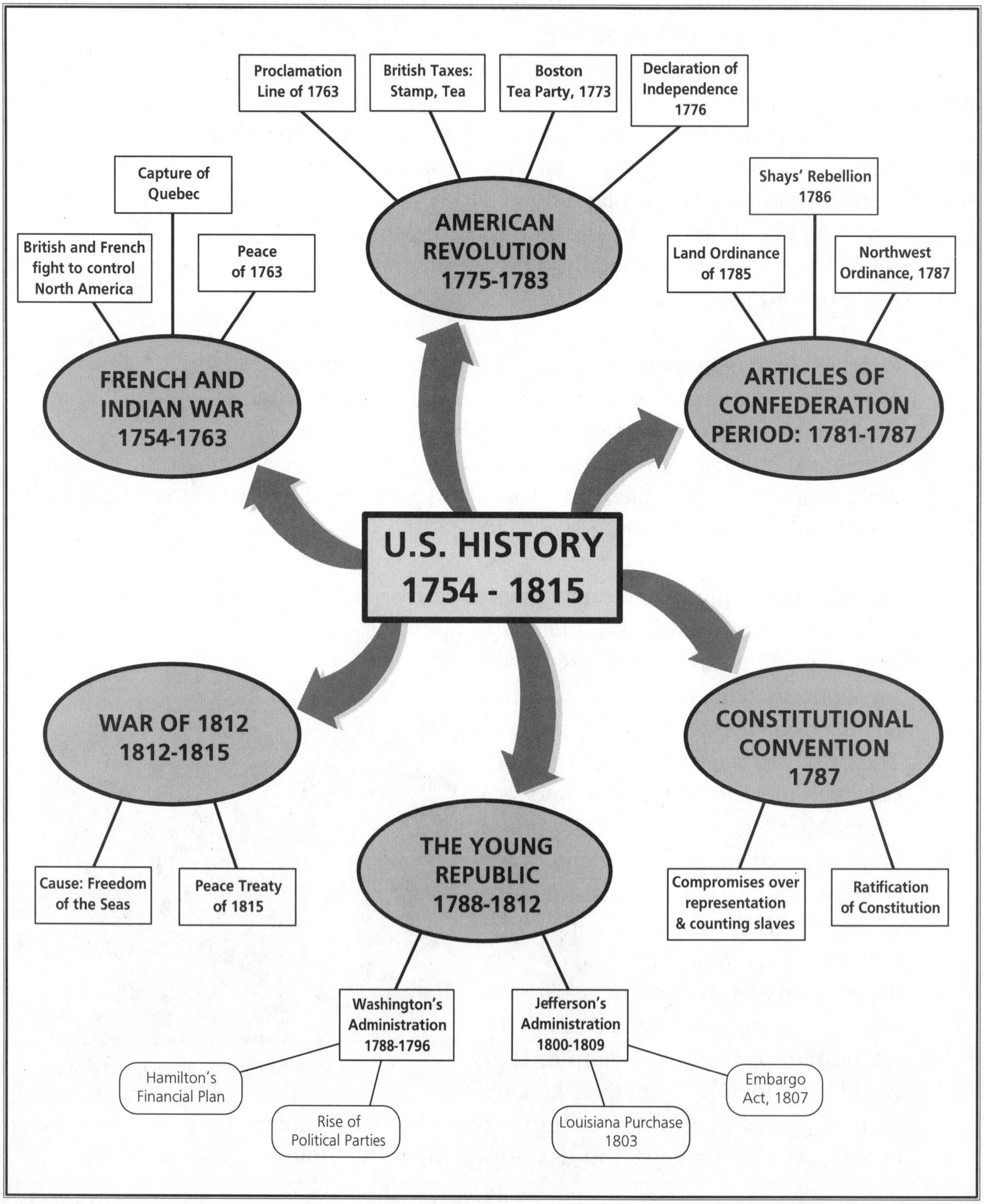

SECTION 3

THE "BIG IDEAS" IN HISTORY

In Chapter 5, you learned that you cannot answer MEAP Test questions correctly simply by interpreting the prompt. You must also understand the "big ideas" included on the test. This section identifies the "big ideas" for history, grouped by standard.

STANDARD I.1: TIME AND CHRONOLOGY

This standard focuses on American history from the American Revolution to the end of the War of 1812. You should know when major events occurred. You should also be able to interpret and construct timelines about this period and know the major factors characterizing this period.

STANDARD I.2: COMPREHENDING THE PAST

This standard requires you to use narratives and graphic data to describe the settings in which major events occurred in the years 1754 to 1815. You must also be able to identify key individuals from this period. You should be able to show how these individuals were affected by their times, how they demonstrated good character, and how they influenced the course of history.

STANDARD: I.3 ANALYZING AND INTERPRETING THE PAST

This standard focuses on how historians use primary and secondary sources to reconstruct past events. Primary sources are the original records of events. Secondary sources are later accounts about an event. Historians often differ in their interpretations of the past. By comparing different interpretations, you should appreciate that our knowledge of the past is subject to change. You should be able to use both primary and secondary sources to analyze significant events in American history. For example, you might be asked to read about the Battle of Lake Erie during the War of 1812, or you might be asked to compare American and British views of that war.

STANDARD: I.4 JUDGING DECISIONS FROM THE PAST

This standard asks you to identify and evaluate decisions made between 1754 and 1815. For these major decisions, you should be able to identify the factors that led to the particular decision and be able to identify alternative courses of action that might have been taken. For example, you should be able to analyze the reasons why Americans decided to replace the Articles of Confederation with a new Constitution. You should also be able to evaluate these decisions in the light of core democratic values. Finally, you should be able to focus on individual responses to violations of human dignity, discrimination, and persecution in this period.

SECTION 4

PRACTICE QUESTIONS

This section contains practice selected-response and constructed-response questions about history. There are two clusters of selected-response questions. Each has a prompt and five questions. There are also two constructed-response questions, each with a prompt and a writing task. Each of these questions has a benchmark number to indicate which "big idea" is being tested. A detailed list of the history benchmarks is found at the end of this chapter.

— SELECTED-RESPONSE QUESTIONS —

Directions: Examine the following map and use it with what you already know to answer the questions that follow.

1 What era of American history does the map depict?

A America at the time of European exploration
B the colonization and settlement of America
C the American Revolution and the birth of the new nation
D the American Civil War and Reconstruction.

I.1.MS.2

2 How did the Northwest Ordinance affect the shaded territory shown on this map?

A It prohibited settlement of this area in order to protect Native Americans.
B It allowed these areas to seek statehood eventually.
C It made this territory independent of Great Britain.
D It provided the peace terms ending the War of 1812.

I.1.MS.2

3 Which type of government did the states in the shaded area of the map adopt?

A oligarchy
B democracy
C constitutional monarchy
D dictatorship

I.1.MS.2

4 If you wanted to learn more about the time period of this map, which of the following SECONDARY sources would you refer to?

A notes by lawmakers about arguments used to pass the Northwest Ordinance
B an encyclopedia article about the Northwest Territory
C the actual Northwest Ordinance passed by Congress
D a diary entry by President George Washington

I.3.MS.1

5 Which is a correct statement about the order of these events?

1. The French and Indian War ends
2. The American Revolution begins
3. The War of 1812 ends

A Events 2 and 3 took place before the establishment of the shaded territory shown in the map.
B Event 1 occurred after the shaded territory in the map was established.
C Event 2 took place while the Northwest Ordinance was being passed.
D Event 3 occurred after the establishment of the shaded territory shown in the map.

I.1.MS.1

Name ______________________ Teacher ______________________

Directions: Read the following passage and use it with what you already know to answer the questions that follow.

THOMAS JEFFERSON (1743-1826)

Thomas Jefferson's impact on America history has been equaled by few others. He served our nation as Governor of Virginia, Ambassador to France, Secretary of State, Vice President, and President of the United States. Despite this impressive list of offices, Jefferson is remembered even more for what he wrote than what he did. He will forever be remembered as the chief author of the Declaration of Independence and his faith in our people's ability to govern themselves.

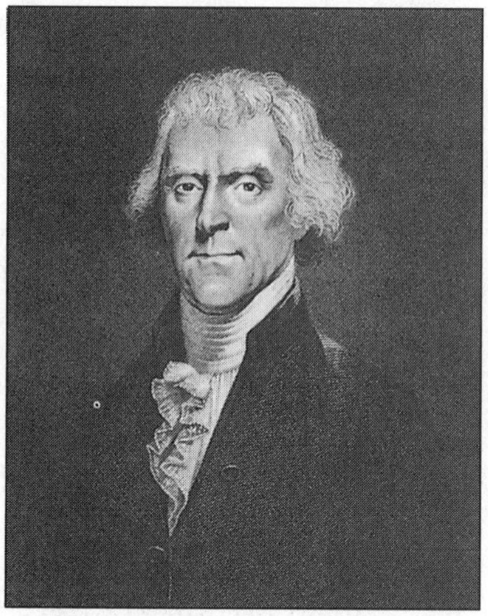
Thomas Jefferson

Jefferson lost in his attempt to succeed George Washington as President in 1796. Four years later, however, Jefferson was elected President. In his Inaugural Address, Jefferson charted a new course for our nation — majority rule, limited government authority, and the protection of individual liberties and minority rights. In his Inaugural Address, he said:

"... [T]hough the will of the majority is in all cases to prevail, that will, to be rightful, must be reasonable; [the] minority possess their equal rights, which equal laws must protect, and [which] to violate would be oppression."

Jefferson's personal life was not without its contradictions. While opposed to the ideas of aristocracy and slavery, he enjoyed a life of great privilege and personally owned slaves.

6 Which of the following would be a SECONDARY source for finding more about the main theme of the reading passage?

A a copy of the Statute of Virginia for Religious Freedom

B the text of the Declaration of Independence

C a recent article about Thomas Jefferson by a modern historian

D a drawing of Monticello by Jefferson

I.3.MS.1

7 Which *core democratic value* is referred to in the quotation from Jefferson's Inaugural Address?

A individual rights

B patriotism

C civilian control of the military

D checks and balances

I.4.MS.4

8 Which of the following events in United States history took place during the lifetime of the subject of this passage?

A Roger Williams founded the Rhode Island colony.

B George Washington became the nation's first President.

C Christopher Columbus landed in the "New World."

D John Smith helped establish a settlement at Jamestown.

I.1.MS.2

9 Which person would have been MOST opposed to the ideas expressed in the documents referred to in Jefferson's Inaugural Address?

A Thomas Paine

B George Washington

C King George III

D Benjamin Franklin

I.2.MS.3

10 Based on the passage, which group might have had reason to question Jefferson's claim to be a genuine democrat and supporter of human rights?

A American farmers

B Federalist Party members

C The British Parliament

D Southern slaves

I.4.MS.3

Name ______________________ Teacher ______________________

— CONSTRUCTED-RESPONSE QUESTIONS —

Following are two constructed-response questions. Read the directions and examine each question carefully before answering. Each question has a benchmark number to show you which "big idea" is being tested.

Directions: You should take about 5 minutes to read the following passage and use it with what you already know to complete this task.

EVENTS LEADING TO AMERICAN INDEPENDENCE

A war broke out between Britain and France for control of North America. The war became known as the **French and Indian War**. The French won several early battles, but the British eventually won the war.

In **1763**, France signed the **Treaty of Paris** agreeing to give up their territory on the North American mainland.

The British decided to impose new taxes on the colonists to pay off debts incurred in defending the colonists from the French. In **1765,** the **Stamp Act** required colonists to use specially stamped paper for newspapers and legal documents. The new taxes greatly angered American colonists. The cry of "no taxation without representation" went up throughout the colonies.

When the British introduced taxes on tea, some colonists dumped British tea into Boston Harbor in the **Boston Tea Party** in **1773**.

Protests finally turned to bloodshed in **1775** when shots were fired between British soldiers and colonists at Lexington and Concord in Massachusetts. Fighting quickly spread to the other colonies, starting the **American Revolutionary War.**

Representatives from the American colonies met in Philadelphia. They decided to break away from Great Britain and declare their independence. The **Declaration of Independence** was issued.

11 There are many ways to understand the unfolding of events in American history. One way is to make a timeline. Finish constructing this timeline (the first event has been done for you) by inserting the five remaining **bolded** events in the reading passage.

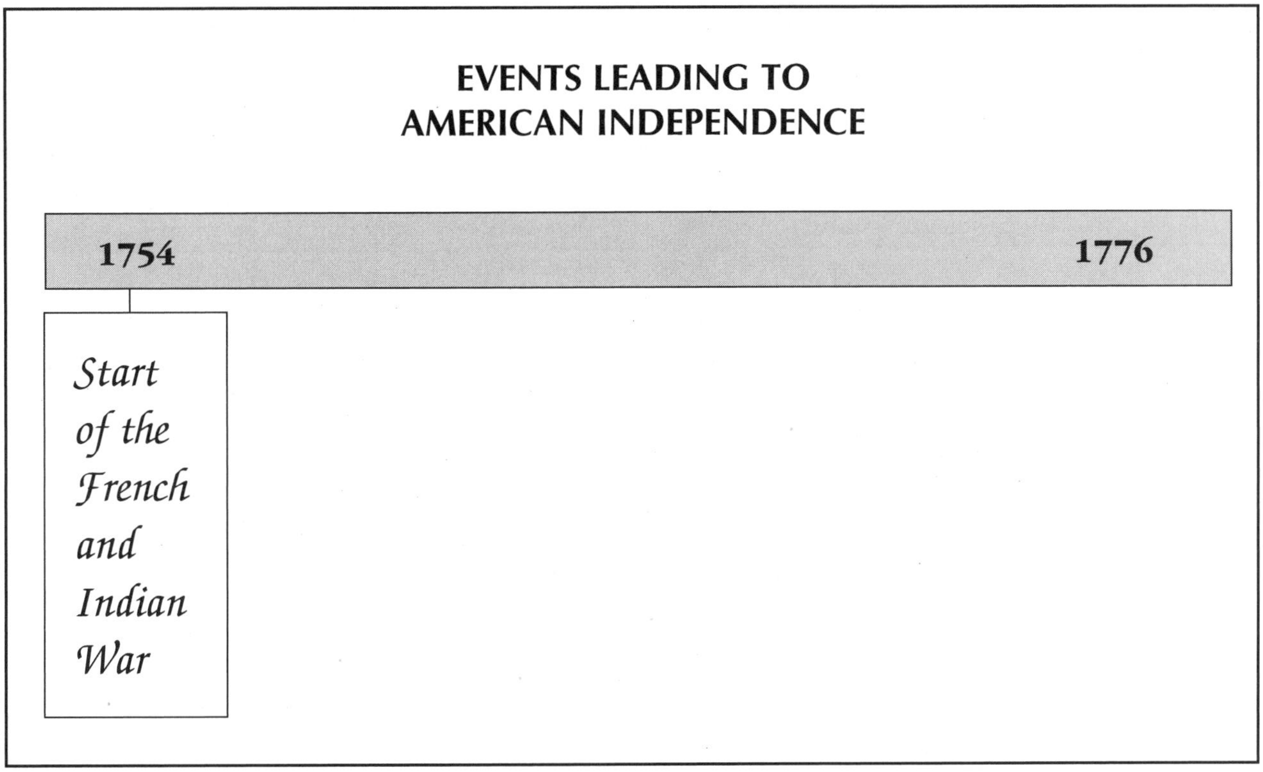

I.1.MS.1

Name ______________________ Teacher ______________________

Directions: You should take about 5 minutes to read the following passage and use it with what you already know to complete this task.

When the delegates first met in Philadelphia on May 25, 1787, they did not realize that they would be spending the next six weeks deciding what would eventually be the new constitution of the United States. During their discussions, they made many compromises. One of these, referred to as the Great Compromise, settled the issue of representation in the new Congress. However, the Great Compromise raised another issue: How should enslaved people be counted for these purposes?

12 On the lines provided, **identify how** the Southern or Northern states wanted to resolve the issue discussed in the passage, and then **explain how** the issue was eventually resolved.

States selected *(circle one)*: Northern states Southern states

Identification of how these states wanted to resolve the issue: ____________________

____

____

____

____

____

Explanation of how the issue was eventually resolved: ____________________

____

____

____

____

____

Name ____________________ Teacher ____________________

BENCHMARKS OF THE HISTORY STRAND

Standard I.1: Time and Chronology

I.1.MS.1 Construct and interpret timelines of people and events from the history of Michigan and the United States through the era of Reconstruction and from the history of other regions of the world. [Note: The MEAP Test will cover up to 1815.]

I.1.MS.2 Describe major factors that characterize the following eras in United States history: the meeting of three worlds (beginnings to 1620), colonization and settlement (1585-1763), Revolution and the new nation (1754-1815), expansion and reform (1801-1861), and the Civil War and Reconstruction (1850-1877). [Note: The MEAP Test will primarily cover 1754 to 1815.]

I.1.MS.3 Select a contemporary condition in Africa, Asia, Canada, Europe and Latin America and trace some of the major historical origins of each.

Standard I.2: Comprehending The Past

I.2.MS.1 Use narratives and graphic data to describe the settings of significant events that shaped the development of Michigan as a state and the United States as a nation during the eras prior to Reconstruction. [Note: The MEAP Test will cover up to 1815.]

I.2.MS.2 Select conditions in various parts of the world and describe how they have been shaped by events from the past.

I.2.MS.3 Use historical biographies to explain how events from the past affected the lives of individuals and how some individuals influenced the course of history.

I.2.MS.4 Identify and explain how individuals in history demonstrated good character and personal virtue.

Standard: I.3 Analyzing and Interpreting the Past

I.3.MS.1 Use primary and secondary records to analyze significant events that shaped the development of Michigan as a state and the United States as a nation prior to the end of the era of Reconstruction. [Note: The MEAP Test will cover up to 1815.]

I.3.MS.2 Analyze interpretations of major events selected from African, Asian, Canadian, European, and Latin American history to reveal the perspectives of the authors.

I.3.MS.3 Show that historical knowledge is tentative and subject to change by describing interpretations of the past that have been revised when new information was uncovered.

I.3.MS.4 Compose narratives of events from the history of Michigan and of the United States prior to the era of Reconstruction.

continued...

Standard: I.4 Judging Decisions from the Past

I.4.MS.1 Identify major decisions in the history of Michigan, and the United States prior to the end of the era of Reconstruction, analyze contemporary factors contributing to the decisions, and consider alternative courses of action. [Note: The MEAP Test will cover up to 1815.]

I.4.MS.2 Identify major decisions in the history of Africa, Asia, Canada, Europe, and Latin America, analyze contemporary factors contributing to the decisions, and consider alternative courses of action.

I.4.MS.3 Identify the responses of individuals to historic violations of human dignity involving discrimination, persecution, and crimes against humanity.

I.4.MS.4 Select historic decisions and evaluate them in light of core democratic values and resulting costs and benefits as viewed from a variety of perspectives.

CHAPTER 8

ECONOMICS

When Kuwaiti oil wells were set ablaze by Iraq in the Gulf War, the price of oil rose because the supply was reduced

The Pentagon in Washington, D.C.; military costs are paid for by taxes

A freighter bringing foreign-made goods to the United States

SECTION 1: A Capsule Summary of Economics

SECTION 2: Major Economics Terms and Concepts

SECTION 3: The "Big Ideas" in Economics

SECTION 4: Practice Questions

SECTION 1 — A CAPSULE SUMMARY OF ECONOMICS

The Social Studies MEAP Test requires you to be familiar with the operation of the United States economy. In particular, you should: (1) understand the basic principles of economics; (2) be able to compare our economic system with others; (3) know how our economic system determines what is produced; (4) understand the important role that the government plays in our economy; and (5) appreciate the effects of world trade. The following summary addresses each of these topics.

THE BASIC PRINCIPLES OF ECONOMICS

THE PROBLEM OF SCARCITY

Most people have unlimited wants. We can never be wholly satisfied because we have only **limited resources** at our disposal to meet these **unlimited wants**. Economists refer to this as the problem of scarcity. For example, everyone in Grand Rapids may want a new home, but there is not enough space, materials, or money available to build such new homes for everyone.

OPPORTUNITY COSTS

Because of the problem of limited resources, whenever we choose to use resources to satisfy one need, we give up the chance to satisfy other needs. This trade-off, in which we give up the opportunity to meet other needs, is known as the **opportunity cost** of an economic choice. For example, if you use your money to buy a new stereo, you give up the opportunity to buy a new computer.

COMPARING OUR ECONOMIC SYSTEM WITH OTHERS

THE THREE BASIC ECONOMIC QUESTIONS

Because of the problem of scarcity, all societies must seek answers to three basic economic questions:

- ***What* should be produced?**
- ***How* should it be produced?**
- ***Who* should get what is produced?**

The method that a society uses to answer these questions is known as its economic system. In general, there are three types of economic systems:

TRADITIONAL ECONOMY

In a traditional economy, the basic economic questions are answered by tradition. People follow the occupations of their ancestors. They farm and make things based on the way their ancestors did. Some families, like nobles, may enjoy special benefits when goods are distributed, simply because their ancestors were privileged in the past.

This farmer plows the same way his father did

COMMAND ECONOMY

In a command economy, the government answers the basic economic questions. Government leaders tell who makes what and who gets it. Modern Communism, as it existed in the Soviet Union between 1917 and 1991, was an example of a command economy.

FREE MARKET ECONOMY

The free market system is based on individual choice rather than tradition or government command. Individuals invest their own money in businesses to produce and sell goods and services so that they will gain a profit. People are free to produce whatever they wish, and to buy whatever they can afford. Government interference in the free market economy is limited. The three basic economic questions are therefore answered by the interplay between **consumers** *(those who buy and use goods and services)* and **producers** *(those who make and sell goods and services)*. The free market system has these features:

Buyers and sellers in an African open-air market

PRIVATE PROPERTY. People have a right to own property and to use it as they see fit.

FREE ENTERPRISE. People are free to take part in any business, buy any product, or sell any legal product. Businesses are also free to do anything they wish to attract customers — such as lower prices, provide better quality, and advertise.

PROFIT MOTIVE. The chance of making profits *(the money that remains after the costs of doing business are paid)* is one of the things that drives people to risk their money in business.

SUPPLY AND DEMAND. The forces of supply and demand eliminate less efficient producers and stop the production of unwanted goods. The interaction of these forces also determines the prices at which goods are sold.

HOW OUR ECONOMIC SYSTEM DETERMINES WHAT IS PRODUCED

THE ROLE OF SUPPLY AND DEMAND

In a free market economy, the basic economic questions are answered by the interaction of consumers and producers. Consumers determine the **demand** for a product. Demand is partly a matter of tastes and preferences, what people can afford, and whether they can substitute other products to meet their needs. If a product becomes too expensive, fewer people are willing to buy it. For example, fewer people will buy a pair of shoes costing $100 than if the same shoes cost $10. Through their buying decisions, consumers determine which products will sell and which will be available.

The price of gasoline often rises and falls because of the interaction of supply and demand

Producers determine the **supply** of a product. They are affected by production costs and the profits they can earn. If the price that consumers will pay for a product increases, producers will make more of it, since they can make more profit. For example, manufacturers are willing to make more shoes if they can sell them for $100 a pair rather than for only $25.

The interaction between what consumers are willing to pay and what producers are willing to sell determines what is produced. The effects of this interaction are sometimes called the **laws of supply and demand**. Here is how the interaction often works in a free market economy:

PRODUCER / CONSUMER INTERACTION

If consumers are willing to pay more for a good or service, then producers will make more of it. This occurs because producers are anxious to increase their profits.	If consumers are not willing to pay as much for a good or service, then producers will have to lower their prices and will not sell as much.	If producers raise their prices, not as many consumers will be willing to buy the product.

ECONOMIC GROUPS AND INSTITUTIONS

An **economic group** is a group of people involved in some economic activity. The American economy depends on many different economic groups and institutions. Each one produces and consumes goods and services.

HOUSEHOLDS

Households act as both consumers and producers. Household members make decisions about where to live, what to eat or wear and what other things to buy. Decisions about productive activities, such as where to work, are also made by household members.

HOUSEHOLD DECISION-MAKING

In making decisions as consumers, household members will usually consider their needs first. They then see what goods and services are available, based on advertising, the experiences of friends, displays in stores, and information available from other sources. Often consumers are influenced by the "brand" name of a product. One good source of information about consumer products is *Consumer Reports*, a monthly magazine that contains impartial comparisons of products, product recommendations, and reports of product reliability. Consumers also consider the price and availability of goods and services when they shop. Often consumers use comparison shopping when making a purchase — shopping for a product in several stores to see which store offers the product at the lowest price.

In making decisions as producers, household members frequently evaluate employment and career opportunities in light of economic trends, past experience, and individual abilities and talents. In our rapidly changing economy, it is likely that many individuals will pursue more than one career in their lifetime. Newspapers, employment agencies, employment advertising, and school counselors are good sources of information about employment and careers.

LABOR UNIONS

Labor unions are organizations of workers whose goal is to get higher wages and better working conditions. At one time there were no unions, and workers labored for long hours in unsafe conditions. Workers found that by forming a labor union and acting together, they had greater influence on their employer. As members of a labor union, workers may strike. A **strike** occurs when union members refuse to work until their demands are met.

Striking workers march at an airline terminal

BUSINESS FIRMS

A business is a unit of production. Small businesses are usually owned by a single individual, a family or small groups of people. Small business owners run their business on a day-to-day basis. Larger businesses are often **corporations**. People form a corporation by investing money in a company. In exchange, they are given a share of the ownership. A large corporation may have thousands of shareholders.

BUSINESS DECISION-MAKING

The aim of a business is to make a **profit**. A business must carefully examine each opportunity to determine whether it will be profitable. Typically, a business must consider the costs of producing or providing a particular good or service. This involves calculating each production cost: raw materials, labor, machinery, space to operate in, etc. The business owner needs to determine if he or she has enough money to invest. Next, the business must determine if there is a market for the product or service, how it will be distributed, and what consumers are willing to pay for it. The business owner also has to consider whether other producers are offering the same good or service, and what they will charge.

To distribute goods, a producer often has several choices. A manufacturer might sell its goods at wholesale prices to retailers like department stores. The store then sells the goods to consumers at higher retail prices. Alternatively, the manufacturer might try to sell its goods to the public directly, or through its own distributors. If the business can keep costs lower than what it receives for selling its products, it will make a profit. Otherwise, it will have a loss and eventually go out of business.

BANKS

Banks are special businesses that hold and protect people's money. People deposit their money in the bank, either in checking accounts or savings accounts. Banks pay depositors interest on their savings accounts. Banks then lend the deposited money out to other people or businesses. For providing this service, banks charge the borrower interest.

A bank branch in a shopping area

THE ROLE OF GOVERNMENT IN A FREE MARKET ECONOMY

Even in a free market system, the government exercises a great deal of influence on the economy. The government prints money, employs workers, and collects taxes. It also acts as a "policeman" in the marketplace. The government makes sure that people and businesses live by the rules and treat each other fairly.

NATIONAL ECONOMIC GOALS

A healthy national economy is important to the well-being of every American. At times, the federal government takes special steps to ensure the smooth running of the American economy. In general, the government has three economic goals:

Promote maximum employment

Promote maximum production

Limit inflation (rising prices)

INSTRUMENTS OF GOVERNMENT ECONOMIC POLICY

To achieve these goals, the federal government has several instruments at its disposal:

- ✦ **The Power To Provide Public Goods**. Governments can provide goods and services by buying them directly. Such products are known as **public goods and services**. Sometimes our federal government uses this power to increase employment or to provide services the economy needs.

- ✦ **The Power to Regulate Economic Activities**. The government takes steps to make sure the marketplace is competitive. It acts as a watchdog over banks, the stock market, and other businesses. Government protects workers and consumers by establishing health and safety standards. It regulates trade by imposing tariffs. It also protects the environment and ensures equal opportunity.

- ✦ **Fiscal Policy**. Government can influence the economy by its spending, taxing, and borrowing policies. In an economic downturn, the government will spend more. By hiring more workers and buying more products, the government creates new jobs. Workers and businesses spend more, increasing demand and stimulating production. This approach was used in the 1930s to fight the Great Depression. On the other hand, if there is a high rate of inflation, government may increase taxes. By collecting more money in taxes than it spends, the government slows down the economy and encourages producers to lower their prices.

✦ **Monetary Policy** is another tool the government uses to stabilize the economy. Monetary policy relies on the government's ability to control the total money supply in our economy. This in turn affects the overall amount of business activity. When money is easily available, interest rates drop. Consumers and businesses borrow more money and make more purchases. The **Federal Reserve Bank**, an agency of the federal government, controls the ability of banks to lend money.

✦ **Taxing Power**. Federal, state, and local governments raise most of the money they need to pay for public goods and services through **taxes** *(money people pay to the government)*. In the United States, taxes have a variety of forms:

MAJOR TYPES OF TAXES IN THE UNITED STATES	
Sales Tax	Tax paid by consumers on their purchases. When a consumer buys a good, a percentage of the sales price is added as a tax. A sales tax is usually charged by state and local governments.
Income Tax	Tax paid on what a person earns yearly from wages and investments. The higher a person's income, the higher the tax rate. This is called a progressive or graduated income tax.
Corporation Tax	A special form of income tax paid by corporations on their profits. It is similar to individual income taxes.
Property Tax	Tax based on the value of property, such as land and buildings. Property taxes are often charged by local governments to pay for school costs.
Customs Duties (tariffs)	Taxes on imports. Sometimes customs duties are used as a protective tariff, raising the cost of imported goods to protect American-made goods from foreign competition.
Social Security Tax	Tax on wages and salaries. Sometimes called FICA, this payroll tax is paid for by both employees and employers. The money collected provides benefits to retired or disabled workers.

Most governments use a combination of these different types of taxes to raise money. However, both the state and federal government must be careful to consider the effects of their tax policies. For example, if one state imposes a large sales tax, residents may simply drive to an adjoining state to make purchases. Sometimes, governments also give special tax breaks to individuals and businesses to encourage certain kinds of investments. Besides collecting taxes, governments frequently borrow money to pay for their spending. Often, governments issue **bonds**, which pay a fixed interest rate to investors who buy them. This borrowing in turn leads to the growth of the **public debt** — the total amount owed by government.

MEASURING THE NATION'S ECONOMIC HEALTH

To measure the health of a national economy, and to compare it with the economies of other nations, economists look at several important statistical indicators. These indicators also influence government leaders in determining national economic policy:

GROSS DOMESTIC PRODUCT (GDP)

This is the value in dollars of all the goods and services produced in a country such as the United States in a single year. Sometimes it is also referred to as the Gross National Product.

PER CAPITA INCOME

This is the Gross Domestic Product divided by the population. It gives us an indication of the average production of a single person.

UNEMPLOYMENT RATE

This measures the number of unemployed people — those who want to work and are actively looking, but cannot find work — divided by the total workforce.

NATIONAL DEBT

This is the total money owed by the government to those who have lent the government money by buying government bonds.

INFLATION RATE

This measures how quickly prices are increasing for the same goods. When everything seems to cost more than a few years ago, this is a sign of inflation. The **Consumer Price Index** (CPI) is sometimes used to keep track of average consumer prices.

INTERNATIONAL TRADE

The American economy is also greatly affected by the world economy and international trade. Increased contact has made nations more interdependent than ever before. Nations are **interdependent** when they depend on trade with one another for goods and services. For example, many American jobs depend on exports. **Exports** are goods and services sold from America to other countries. The United States also depends on imports. **Imports** are products from other countries brought into the United States for sale.

WHY NATIONS TRADE

Most nations do not produce everything they need. As a result, nations trade with other nations to obtain many products. Because countries have different locations, climates, and natural resources, some nations can produce certain goods at a lower cost or more efficiently than other nations can. The soil and climate of Colombia, for example, gives it an advantage over others in growing coffee beans.

A tanker brings foreign oil to the United States

SPECIALIZATION

In general, nations prosper by specializing — putting their money, resources, and labor into making the things at which they are most efficient. Each country is generally better off trading those products it makes best and using the money it gets to buy different goods and services from other nations that produce these other goods at lower cost. All countries benefit as a result.

GOVERNMENT REGULATION

Our Constitution gives the federal government the power to regulate trade between states and with other countries — referred to as **interstate and foreign commerce**. The federal government, for example, inspects products entering the United States to make sure they are safe. Products made abroad must be clearly marked to show where they were made. Sometimes the federal government also imposes **tariffs**, special taxes on goods imported from abroad. Because the United States favors trade without tariffs, it has made agreements such as North American Free Trade Agreement (NAFTA) that aim at lowering tariffs.

MONEY AND THE EXCHANGE OF GOODS

One of the most important functions of money is to act as a medium of exchange. In earliest times, merchants traded by **barter** — they simply exchanged goods. In later times, merchants from different regions traded goods for coins made of **precious metals** like gold and silver. Later, they used paper **currency** *(money)* backed by gold for exchange. When one country held too much currency from another country, it would simply redeem this currency in gold. Today, international trade is based on the exchange of paper money backed by the promises of individual governments.

New paper money being inspected at the U.S. Mint

SECTION 2 MAJOR ECONOMIC TERMS AND CONCEPTS

Use this graphic organizer to review your understanding of important economics terms and concepts.

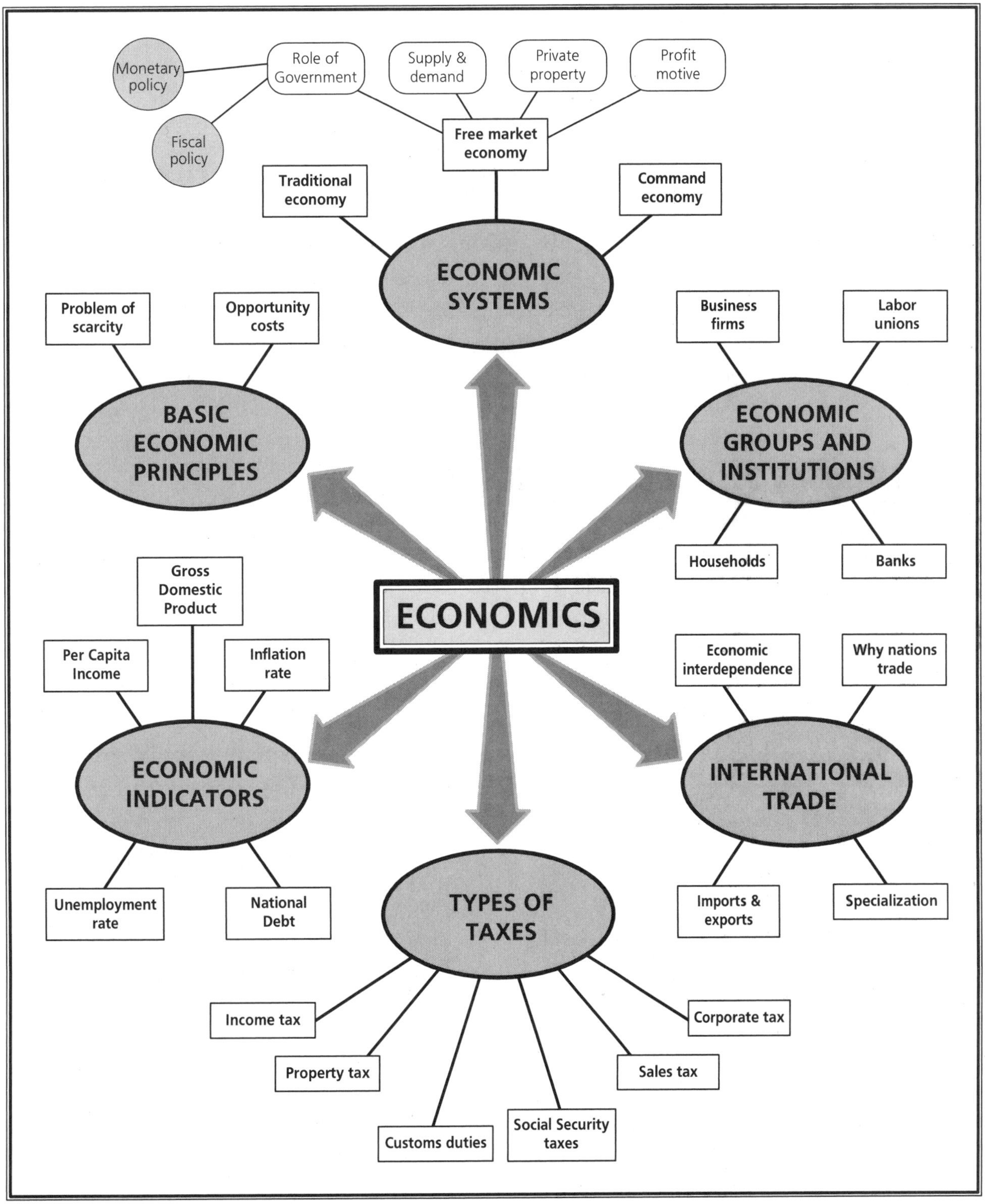

SECTION 3

THE "BIG IDEAS" IN ECONOMICS

Prompts are used to test your understanding of the "big ideas" in social studies. This section summarizes the "big ideas" for economics, grouped by standard.

STANDARD IV.1: INDIVIDUAL AND HOUSEHOLD CHOICES

This standard looks at how individuals and households make economic decisions in a free market economy. You should be able to use economic reasoning to compare the prices, quality, and features of various goods and services. You should also be able to evaluate employment and career opportunities in light of changing economic trends. Finally, you should be able to analyze the reliability of the information you receive when making typical economic decisions.

STANDARD IV.2: BUSINESS CHOICES

This standard examines how businesses make choices in organizing, producing, and using resources. You should be able to give a real example of how a business operates and how an entrepreneur makes a profit. You should also be able to compare various methods for the production and distribution of goods and services. For example, how did Ford's assembly-line method compare with earlier methods of automobile production? How does Amway's method of distributing goods today compare with more traditional methods of retailing? Finally, you should be able to explain how businesses are affected by current public policies — such as taxes or spending on public goods.

Ford assembly line, 1914

Ford assembly line, 1990s

STANDARD IV.3: ROLE OF GOVERNMENT

This standard focuses on how government decisions affect the economy — especially decisions on taxation, public spending, public goods, and regulation. You should be able to distinguish between private and public goods, and to provide examples of each. You should be able to identify different indicators the government uses to measure the functioning of our economy, such as the Gross Domestic Product, inflation, and the unemployment rate. You should be able to distinguish different forms of taxation, such as income tax and sales tax, and to compare their effects. Finally, you should be able to furnish specific case studies to assess the role of the government in the economy.

STANDARD IV.4: ECONOMIC SYSTEMS

This standard focuses on how a free market system works. You should know how producers and consumers interact to determine both what is produced and the prices at which goods and services are sold. You should be able to describe the roles that various economic groups and institutions play in the American economy, such as governments, business firms, banks, labor unions, and households. Finally, you should be able to explain how consumers obtain information about available goods and services from advertising and other sources to make informed decisions.

The meat-packing industry, a part of the American free market economy

STANDARD IV.5: TRADE

This standard focuses on the role of national and international trade in the economy. You should be able to explain how different national and world regions contribute to world trade. For example, the Great Lakes region is an important center for food processing and automobile manufacturing. The region therefore produces more cereal and automobiles than its own population needs. It exchanges those products for goods and services from other regions. You should also be able to explain the role of the federal government in regulating interstate and international trade. Finally, you should be able to describe the historical development of means of payment between nations, such as use of the gold standard, making international trade possible.

SECTION 4 — PRACTICE QUESTIONS

This section contains selected-response and constructed-response questions about economics. There are two clusters of selected-response questions, each with a prompt and five questions. Examine each prompt carefully and answer the questions. There are also two constructed-response questions, each with a prompt and a writing task. After examining the prompt, write your answers as directed. Each question has the benchmark number of the "big idea" being tested.

— SELECTED-RESPONSE QUESTIONS —

Directions: Examine the following photographs and use them with what you already know to answer the questions that follow:

Photograph 1

Photograph 4

Photograph 2

Photograph 5

Photograph 3

Photograph 6

1 The scene shown in photograph 2 best illustrates which economic concept?

A traditional economy

B global interdependence

C natural resources

D consumer credit

IV.5.MS.1

2 Economic activities often found in a traditional economy are illustrated by which pair of photographs?

A Photographs 1 and 4

B Photographs 2 and 6

C Photographs 1 and 2

D Photographs 3 and 4

IV.4.MS.1

3 In which area of the world would the person working in photograph 5 MOST likely be found?

A Amazon rain forest

B Sahara Desert

C European plains

D African savanna

IV.4.MS.1

4 What is the MOST logical conclusion that can be drawn about the economy of the nation shown in photograph 3?

A It must be a command economy.

B It has a highly industrialized work force.

C It is probably a traditional economy.

D It is a high-tech economy.

IV.2.MS.4

5 In which photograph would you expect to find the barter system of exchange being used?

A Photograph 1

B Photograph 2

C Photograph 4

D Photograph 5

IV.5.MS.3

Name ______________________ Teacher ______________________

Directions: Study the following chart and use it with what you already know to answer the questions that follow.

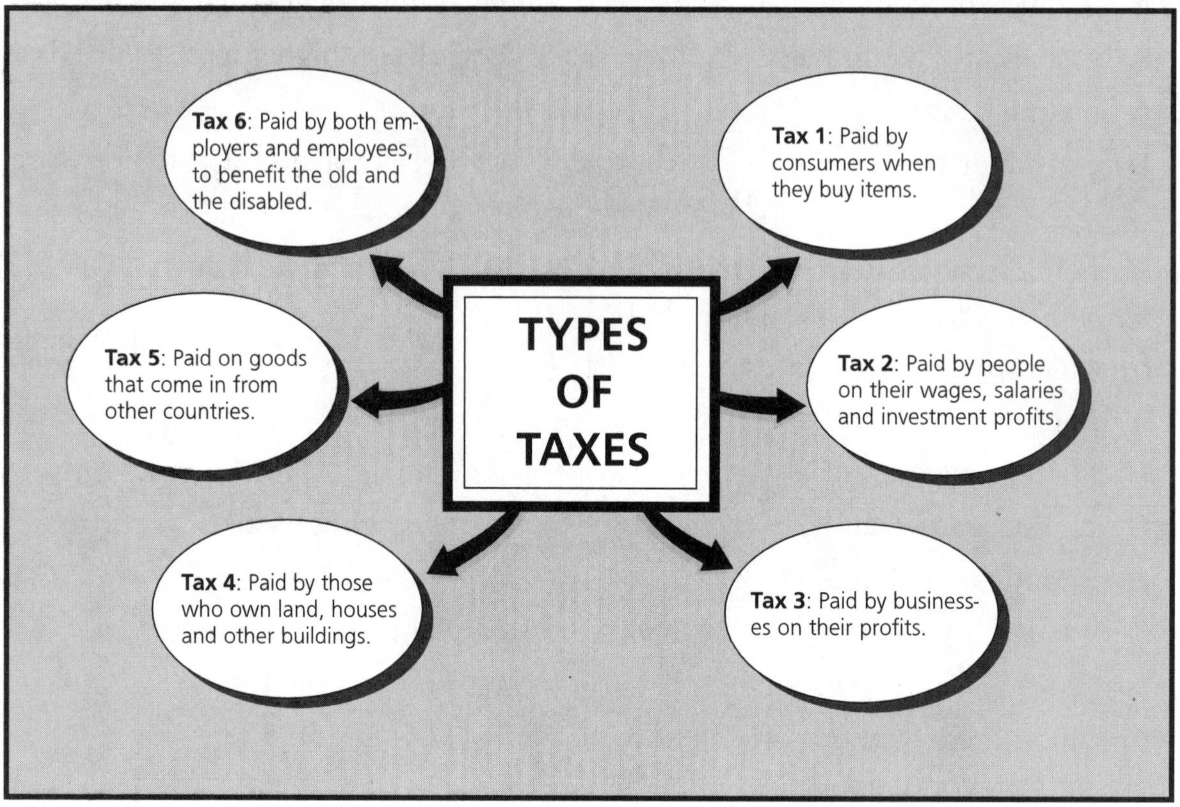
Tax 6: Paid by both employers and employees, to benefit the old and the disabled.
Tax 1: Paid by consumers when they buy items.
TYPES OF TAXES
Tax 5: Paid on goods that come in from other countries.
Tax 2: Paid by people on their wages, salaries and investment profits.
Tax 4: Paid by those who own land, houses and other buildings.
Tax 3: Paid by businesses on their profits.

6 What is a MAIN purpose of Tax 5?

A to provide money for government programs aiding senior citizens

B to stimulate spending by American consumers

C to protect American products against competing foreign goods

D to encourage people to behave in a certain way

IV.5.MS.2

7 The State of Michigan needs additional money for the coming year. It wants to raise taxes to supply this money. Which two taxes could it legally use to raise the money?

A Taxes 1 and 2

B Taxes 2 and 5

C Taxes 4 and 6

D Taxes 5 and 6

IV.5.MS.2

8 Which tax is generally used by government to reduce the gap between rich and poor people?

A Tax 1

B Tax 2

C Tax 3

D Tax 5

IV.5.MS.2

9 You have just moved to a state that has a sales tax and an income tax. You have rented an apartment and have begun working for the ABC Importing Corporation. In the course of the year, what type of taxes would you expect to pay?

A Taxes 1, 2 and 6

B Taxes 1, 2, 3 and 6

C Taxes 1, 2, 3, 4, and 6

D Taxes 1, 4, 5, and 6

IV.3.MS.3

10 The economy of the United States is facing a slowdown. Many businesses are failing and unemployment is rising. Which action by the federal government would stimulate the nation's economy by putting more money into the hands of consumers?

A increase Tax 3

B decrease Tax 5

C decrease Tax 2

D increase Tax 6

IV.3.MS.3

Name ______________________ Teacher ______________________

— CONSTRUCTED-RESPONSE QUESTIONS —

Following are two constructed-response questions. Read the directions and examine each question carefully before answering. Each question has a benchmark number to show which "big idea" is being tested.

Directions: You should take about 5 minutes to read the following material and use it with what you already know to complete this task.

An economic group is a group involved in some economic activity. Our society has many different kinds of economic groups.

KEY GROUPS IN THE AMERICAN ECONOMY

Households	Small Businesses	Banks
Labor Unions	Large Corporations	Government

11 On the lines provided, describe the role of **one** economic group listed above in the American economy.

Economic group selected: ______________________________

Description of the role of that economic group: ______________________

____

____

____

____

____

IV.4.MS.2

Name ______________________ Teacher ______________________

Directions: You should take about 5 minutes to read the following and use it with what you already know to complete this task.

Economists, business owners, and consumers often rely on a number of measures that let them know the condition of the American economy. Such measures are called indicators. The best known indicators include:

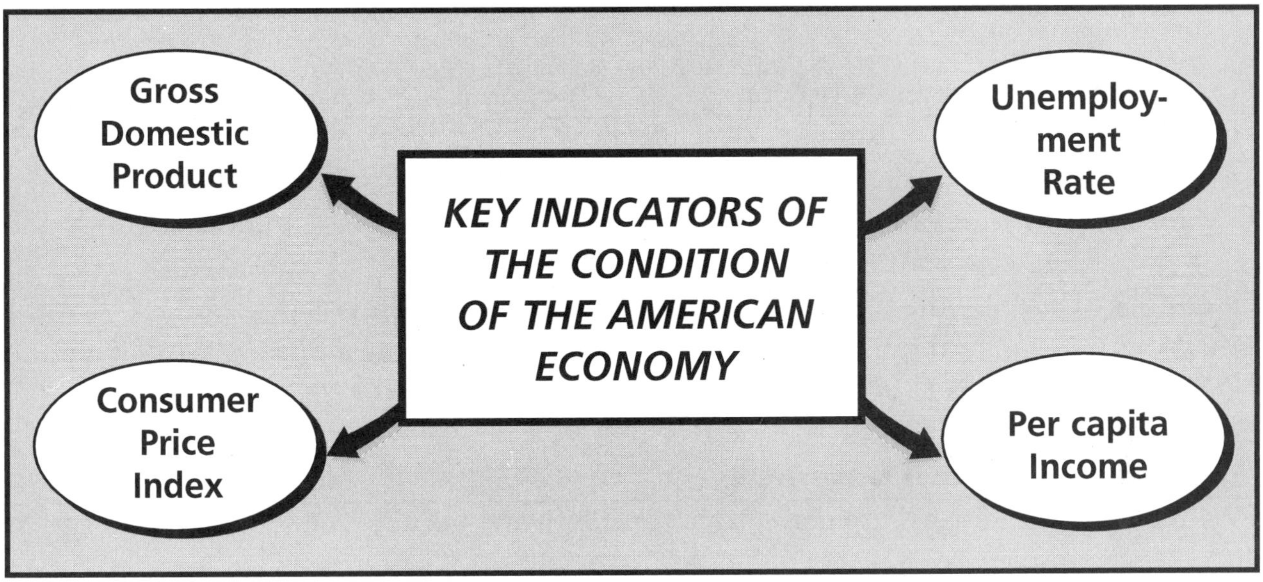

12 On the lines provided, select **one** indicator of the American economy and describe what it shows.

Name of indicator selected: ______________________________

Description of what it shows: ______________________________

____

____

____

____

____

____

IV.4.MS.2

Name ______________________ Teacher ______________________

BENCHMARKS OF THE ECONOMICS STRAND

Standard IV.1: Individual and Household Choices

IV.1.MS.1 Use economic reasoning when comparing prices, quality, and features of goods and services.

IV.1.MS.2 Evaluate employment and career opportunities in light of economic trends.

IV.1.MS.3 Analyze the reliability of information when making economic decisions.

Standard IV.2: Business Choices

IV.2.MS.1 Using a real example, describe how business practices, profits and a willingness to take risks, enable an entrepreneur to operate.

IV.2.MS.2 Compare various methods for the production and distribution of goods and services.

IV.2.MS.3 Describe the effects of a current public policy on businesses.

IV.2.MS.4 Examine the historical and contemporary role an industry has played and continues to play in a community.

Standard IV.3: Role of Government

IV.3.MS.1 Distinguish between public and private goods using contemporary examples.

IV.3.MS.2 Identify and describe different forms of economic measurement.

IV.3.MS.3 Use case studies to assess the role of government in the economy.

IV.3.MS.4 Distinguish different forms of taxation and describe their effects.

Standard IV.4: Economic Systems

IV.4.MS.1 Compare the historical record of market and command economies in solving the problem of scarcity.

IV.4.MS.2 Describe the roles of the various economic institutions which comprise the American economic system such as governments, business firms, labor unions, banks, and households.

IV.4.MS.3 Use case studies to exemplify how supply and demand, prices, incentives, and profits determine what is produced and distributed in the American economy.

IV.4.MS.4 Analyze how purchasers obtain information about goods and services from advertising and other sources.

Standard IV.5: Trade

IV.5.MS.1 Identify the current and potential contributions of national and world regions to trade.

IV.5.MS.2 Examine the role of the United States government in regulating commerce as stated in the United States Constitution.

IV.5.MS.3 Describe the historical development of the different means of payment such as barter, precious metals, or currency to facilitate exchange.

CHAPTER 9

CIVICS

John F. Kennedy campaigning for President, 1960

A citizen votes in an election

Reagan-Mondale debate in the 1984 campaign

SECTION 1

A CAPSULE SUMMARY OF CIVICS

The Social Studies MEAP Test for grade 8 requires you to be familiar with the constitutional foundations of American government. You should know: (1) what government is; (2) the basic principles of American government; (3) the role of law and individual rights; (4) how public officials are chosen; and (5) America's role in world affairs. The following summary addresses each of these topics.

WHAT IS GOVERNMENT?

People are social beings: they need to live with others in groups or communities. As a result, communities need to make rules to settle disagreements among their members and to protect the community from those who violate its rules. The organization set up to protect the community is called **government**. Just as a pilot guides a ship, a government guides the members of a community in their dealings with themselves and outsiders. All governments are given powers to carry out their authority over the members of society. These powers include:

- **a *legislative* power to make the laws**
- **an *executive* power to carry out the laws**
- **a *judicial* power to interpret the laws**

Governmental authority is a matter of great concern to each of us. Why do we give people whom we hardly know such power over our lives? And how much power can we give to our government without allowing it to threaten our liberties? These questions help us to appreciate the difficulties that faced the authors of our system of government more than 200 years ago.

CONSTITUTIONAL PRINCIPLES

To create a balanced system of government that would provide order without threatening individual liberties, the members of the Constitutional Convention — who created our present system of government — adopted the following principles:

POPULAR SOVEREIGNTY

The U.S. Constitution is based on the concept of **popular sovereignty** — the people decide what they want by majority rule. This principle is stated in the **Preamble** *(introduction)* to the Constitution. Its opening words, "We, the People ...," tell us that our system of government was created by the citizens themselves. The authors of the Constitution acted as the representatives of the American people. The Constitution established a government of elected officials in order to keep supreme political power in the hands of the people.

This system of democratic government differs from other forms of government, such as a **dictatorship**, in which one person or a small group holds all political power and citizens have few rights. Our system also differs from a **monarchy**, in which a ruler holds power through inherited right.

The rest of the Preamble identifies what its authors believed should be the goals of our national government. These are shown on the scroll to the right.

> *We, the People of the United States,*
> - *in order to form a more perfect Union,*
> - *establish justice,*
> - *ensure domestic tranquillity,*
> - *provide for the common defense,*
> - *promote the general welfare,*
> - *and secure the blessings of liberty to ourselves and our posterity,*
>
> *do ordain and establish this Constitution for the United States of America.*

FEDERALISM

The writers of the Constitution feared giving too much power to the central government. Instead, they balanced governmental power between the national government and the thirteen state governments. To do this, they created a system called **federalism**, where power was shared. Our national government deals with matters that affect the whole country. State governments mainly handle affairs relating to individual states.

SUPREMACY OF THE NATIONAL GOVERNMENT

The framers of the Constitution realized that there were bound to be future conflicts between the national *(federal)* government and the state governments. Anticipating such conflicts, they added the **Supremacy Clause**. This clause states that the Constitution is the highest law in the land. Just below the Constitution are federal laws, which are superior to any conflicting state laws.

LIMITED GOVERNMENT

The Constitution takes great care to *limit* government power by spelling out the specific powers of the federal government. The federal government can only use those powers that are given to it in the Constitution itself. These are known as **delegated powers**. For example, Congress has the power to coin money. However, one important clause, sometimes known as the **elastic clause**, allows Congress to expand or stretch its powers in some situations. This clause gives Congress the power to enact laws that it deems "necessary and proper" for accomplishing any of its other powers.

SEPARATION OF POWERS

Because the authors of the Constitution feared leaving too much power in the hands of any one government, they also **separated** the three main powers of government into different branches — the **legislative branch**, the **executive branch**, and the **judicial branch**. They believed this separation would make it difficult for any one person or branch of government to become too powerful. State governments, like Michigan, also follow the same model of separating powers among three branches.

SEPARATION OF POWERS

LEGISLATIVE BRANCH	EXECUTIVE BRANCH	JUDICIAL BRANCH
Power to make the laws	*Power to carryout the laws*	*Power to interpret the laws*

	LEGISLATIVE POWER	EXECUTIVE POWER	JUDICIAL POWER
NATIONAL GOVERNMENT	Congress	President	Supreme Court
STATE OF NEW YORK	State Legislature	Governor	Court of Appeals
STATE OF MICHIGAN	State Legislature	Governor	Supreme Court

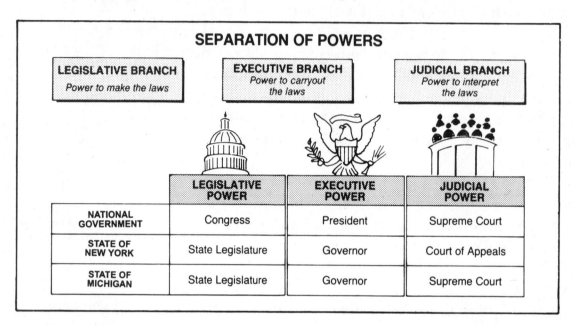

CHECKS AND BALANCES

As a final way to make sure that no branch of the federal government becomes too powerful, the Constitution gives each branch ways to "check" *(limit)* the powers of the other branches. For example, the U.S. Senate must approve most Presidential appointments. On the other hand, the President can veto *(refuse to sign)* laws that Congress passes. Congress can override a veto, but only if two-thirds of the House and Senate vote in favor of the override. Power was "balanced" among the branches so that important actions could not be taken unless there was a general agreement.

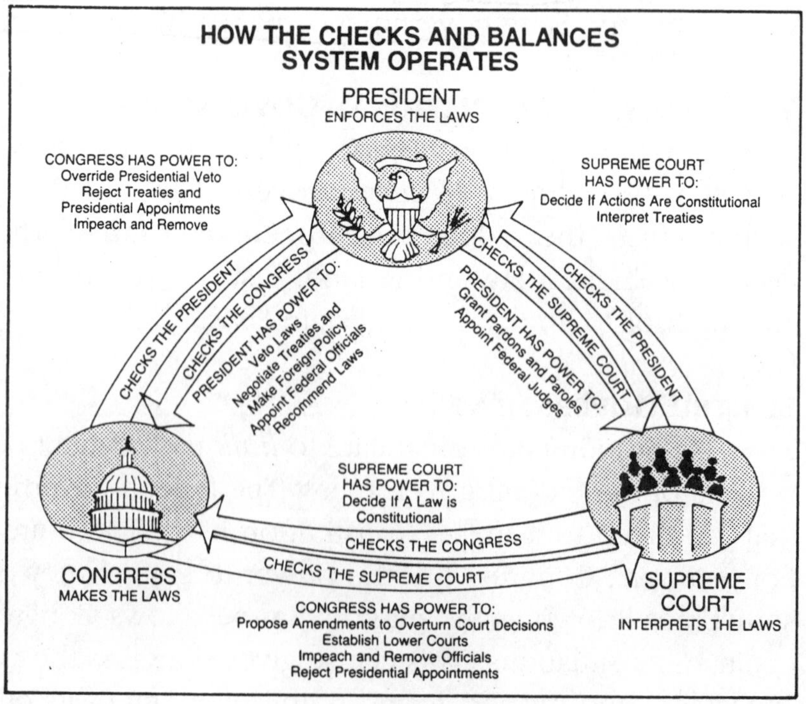

WHO MAKES FOREIGN POLICY?

A good example of the separation of powers and checks and balances can be seen in the way the Constitution handles foreign policy. **Foreign policy** is the conduct of one nation towards other nations. The Constitution divides control over foreign policy between the President and Congress. The President has the day-to-day control of foreign policy. The President's foreign policy powers include:

President Lyndon Johnson (left) with General Westmoreland during the Vietnam War

- ✦ serving as Commander-in-Chief of the armed forces
- ✦ negotiating treaties
- ✦ appointing ambassadors and receiving foreign ministers

But the Constitution also gives Congress some important foreign policy powers. This was done primarily to create a "check" or control on the President. The foreign policy powers of Congress include:

- ✦ declaring war
- ✦ approving treaties and Presidential appointments
- ✦ deciding how much the President may spend on national defense

Generally, the President's ability to act quickly has allowed the Presidency to become the main force in making United States foreign policy. However, Congress has often attempted to control foreign policy, especially at the end of major conflicts or crises.

FLEXIBILITY

Although it was written over 200 years ago, the Constitution has been able to keep up with the changing needs of our country. Changing interpretations of the Constitution by the U.S. Supreme Court help adapt the Constitution to new conditions. The Constitution also keeps pace through the process of **amendment** *(changes or additions to the Constitution)*. It is much more difficult to amend the Constitution, however, than to pass an ordinary law. Three-quarters of the states must agree to the amendment. This is because the Constitution is superior to any other law and should not be changed easily. The first ten amendments to the Constitution are known as the **Bill of Rights**, and protect our individual liberties.

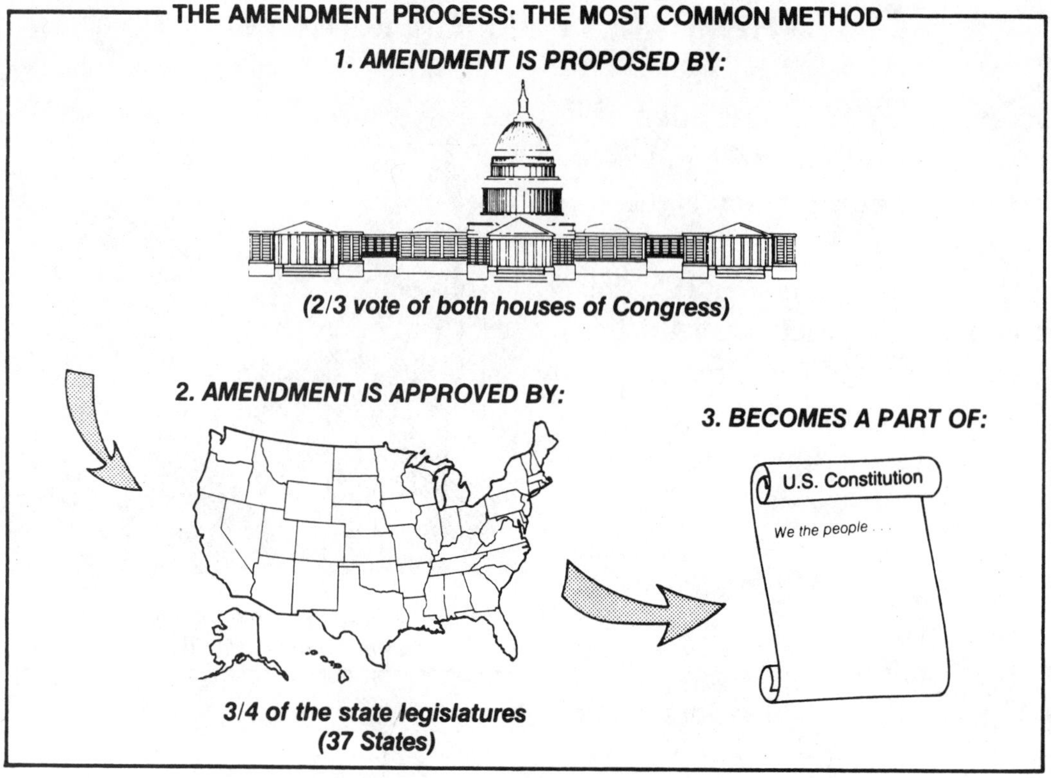
THE AMENDMENT PROCESS: THE MOST COMMON METHOD
1. AMENDMENT IS PROPOSED BY:
(2/3 vote of both houses of Congress)
2. AMENDMENT IS APPROVED BY:
3/4 of the state legislatures
(37 States)
3. BECOMES A PART OF:
U.S. Constitution
We the people . . .

THE RULE OF LAW

Another very important principle of the American system of government is the "rule of law." A **law** tells people what they must do or not do. Usually there is a **penalty** *(punishment)* for breaking the law. Because we have a written set of laws, each of us is subject to the same rules. Government officials cannot fine or imprison us unless we break those laws. This promotes fairness and equality.

In our democracy, laws are made for the public by their elected representatives. There are several law-making bodies in our system of government. The ones most familiar to you are probably the **U.S. Congress** and the **Michigan State Legislature**. Your county or town may also have a law-making body.

What Do Courts Do?

No law can be so precise that it can foresee all situations that may arise. For this reason, we need courts to apply the law to particular situations. First of all, there may be factual questions about what really happened. Second, there are often questions about how the law should be applied. A **trial court** hears each side present its case and reviews the evidence. It then interprets the words of the law to see if the law applies to that situation. For example:

A sign may read **No Vehicles In The Park.** We are fairly sure this means no cars or trucks are allowed in the park, but what about bicycles? Suppose we decide that bicycles are banned because they are a danger to pedestrians. Then what about baby strollers or wheelchairs?

OUR FEDERAL SYSTEM OF JUSTICE

In general, courts handle both criminal and civil cases. In a **criminal case**, the defendant is accused of breaking the law and may be sent to jail or forced to pay a fine. In a **civil case**, people ask the court to resolve some dispute. One party might claim that the other party owes money because it violated its contract or caused an injury through negligence. Civil and criminal trials follow different procedures. For example, in some civil cases a party may not be entitled to a trial by jury.

Federal courts only try cases involving federal law or disputes between citizens from different states. **Appeals courts** have a different function than trial courts. When a trial court gives its verdict, the parties can appeal the decision to an appeals court. The appeals court reviews the issues of law, not the facts of the case, to see if the law was applied correctly. If they decide the law was misapplied, they can overturn the decision. Then the case usually goes back to the trial court for a retrial.

THE ROLE OF THE SUPREME COURT

The U.S. Supreme Court is the country's highest "Court of Appeals," and hears appeals from federal and state courts. After a law is passed by Congress, if a dispute arises over the meaning of the law, it can be appealed to the Supreme Court. The Supreme Court can reject any law it believes would violate the U.S. Constitution. This power to decide the constitutionality of a law is known as **judicial review**. The only way to override a ruling by the Supreme Court that a law is unconstitutional is to pass an amendment to the Constitution. Because the Supreme Court can declare laws unconstitutional, it has a special role in protecting the individual rights guaranteed in the U.S. Constitution.

The chamber in which the U.S. Supreme Court hears cases

THE BILL OF RIGHTS

When the Constitution was first written, it contained no Bill of Rights. The Bill of Rights was added to the Constitution in 1791, in the form of the first ten amendments.

THE FIRST AMENDMENT

The First Amendment guarantees that Congress cannot pass a law taking away the freedom of religion, free speech, freedom of the press, freedom to assemble, or the freedom to ask government officials to change the laws. These freedoms are not unlimited. For example, freedom of speech does not mean we have the right to say whatever we want in all circumstances. A person cannot yell "Fire!" in a crowded movie theater as a joke. This would endanger people's lives. However, the Supreme Court usually denies most attempts by government to limit freedom of speech. Restriction of free speech is justified only if a real threat of danger currently exists.

AMENDMENTS ON THE RIGHTS OF THE ACCUSED

Our public officials hold tremendous power. They can search our homes, put us in jail, and, in extreme cases, take our lives. Because of these powers, the Bill of Rights devoted the Fourth, Fifth, Sixth, and Eighth Amendments to limiting the way officials could use their powers. These amendments prohibit government officials from taking a person's life, liberty, or property without fair and reasonable legal procedures. These procedures are known as the "**due process of law.**" Some of these protections are identified in the graphic organizer that follows:

Fourth Amendment: A person's property cannot be searched or taken away by the authorities without fair and reasonable legal procedures.

Fifth Amendment: People are not required to give evidence against themselves. The Supreme Court has also ruled that people in police custody must be informed of their constitutional rights before being questioned.

Sixth Amendment: People accused of a crime must have a fair and impartial trial. They must be told of the charges against them. In criminal trials, they have the right to a jury and to be represented by a lawyer.

Eighth Amendment: Courts cannot punish a convicted person in a cruel or unusual way.

FOURTEENTH AMENDMENT

When it was first passed, the Bill of Rights protected individuals from the actions of the *federal* government, but not from actions by *state* governments. After the Civil War, Congress passed the **Fourteenth Amendment** (1868), to protect citizens from abuses by state governments. It accomplished this in two ways:

- ✦ **Due Process Rights.** State governments must follow the same procedures as the federal government when arresting, searching, and convicting persons accused of a crime. States cannot take away freedom of expression except for the same narrow reasons that the federal government can.

- ✦ **Equal Protection Rights.** The Fourteenth Amendment also guarantees "equal protection" of the laws. This means state governments cannot treat some groups differently from others unless there is an overriding reason. For example, a state government can refuse to allow three-year olds the right to vote because it is overwhelmingly clear that three-year olds are not mature enough to vote. But a state government cannot refuse to let some people vote because of their race or ethnic background.

ACHIEVING AMERICAN IDEALS

The realities of life in the United States have not always lived up to the promise of American ideals, reflected in such documents as the Declaration of Independence and the U.S. Constitution. For example, despite amendments guaranteeing voting rights, many African Americans in Southern states were long denied the right to vote. Beginning in the early 1900s, the leaders of many disadvantaged groups, especially African Americans and women, organized reform movements to improve their conditions and to create an environment that would be free of discrimination.

Suffragists marching in 1912. Women struggled from 1848 to 1920 to gain the right to vote.

- ✦ **Nineteenth Amendment** (1920). This guaranteed women the right to vote throughout the United States.

- ✦ **Brown v. Board of Education of Topeka.** After World War II, the Supreme Court sought to protect people from state and local governments taking away their civil rights and to ensure that all citizens had a right to the equal protection of the law. In 1954, the Supreme Court ruled that racial segregation (*the separation of blacks and whites*) in public schools was unconstitutional because separate schools were by their very nature unequal. The case marked an important turning point in ending segregated schools.

Public places were often segregated before the Civil Rights Movement, as this photo shows.

- ✦ **Affirmative Action Programs**. In 1965, President Lyndon B. Johnson signed an order requiring employers with federal contracts to make sure that they hired minority and female employees. Affirmative action programs increased minority and female representation in colleges, the professions, and in many businesses and occupations. However, many cities and states have begun ending affirmative action programs because of the tremendous advances that minorities and women have made over the past 30 years.

✦ **From the Civil Rights Act to the Americans with Disabilities Act**. Starting in 1964, Congress also passed a series of laws prohibiting discrimination against disadvantaged groups — women, Native Americans, Hispanic Americans, and the disabled. In 1990, Congress passed an act guaranteeing that disabled people will be treated equally in their jobs and be given easy access to office buildings, stores, restaurants, stadiums, trains, and buses.

HOW OUR PUBLIC OFFICIALS ARE CHOSEN

An essential characteristic of democracy is that citizens are able to choose their own representatives. Under our system, officials at the local, state, and national levels get their jobs either by being elected or appointed.

THE ROLE OF POLITICAL PARTIES

Political parties have become an essential part of our system of government. They bring together people who share common principles and want to see particular policies and programs adopted. Political parties try to accomplish this by getting their members elected to public office. Political parties are **not** mentioned in the Constitution. The framers of the Constitution purposely omitted political parties because they hoped to create a unified nation, free from disunity and division. But soon after the ratification of the Constitution, differences between Alexander Hamilton and Thomas Jefferson led them to form the first American political parties. Hamilton's followers became known as **Federalists**, while Jefferson's supporters were called **Democratic-Republicans**. Today, political parties perform several important functions in our democratic system:

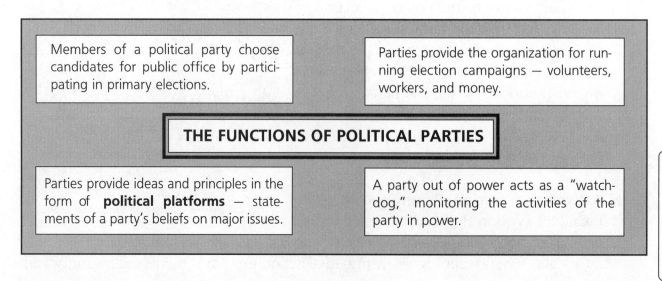

Members of a political party choose candidates for public office by participating in primary elections.

Parties provide the organization for running election campaigns — volunteers, workers, and money.

THE FUNCTIONS OF POLITICAL PARTIES

Parties provide ideas and principles in the form of **political platforms** — statements of a party's beliefs on major issues.

A party out of power acts as a "watchdog," monitoring the activities of the party in power.

The Role of Elections

Each party nominates candidates to present to voters. The party helps to stimulate voter interest in their candidates. They work for the nomination and election of their candidates through an election campaign, in which candidates present themselves to the voters. Party members and campaign volunteers criticize opposition candidates, and provide money to pay for pamphlets, signs, newspaper and television advertising, and campaign events.

Ronald Reagan accepting the nomination for President at the Republican National Convention in 1984

In evaluating candidates for public office, it is important to consider what they promise to achieve, their experience and ability, and their past record. Voters obtain information about candidates from several sources:

- listening to candidates' speeches;
- reading statements released by the candidates;
- listening to the views of friends and relatives as well as of professional commentators;
- watching candidates debate each other on the issues; and
- following the election campaign in newspapers, magazines, and on television.

Voters choose from among several candidates on **election day**, when they cast their votes. In most elections, the candidate with the most votes wins. He or she will fill a public position for a fixed term, after which another election will be held.

AMERICAN GOVERNMENT AND WORLD AFFAIRS

Our federal government represents us in world affairs. Just as citizens in the United States sometimes have conflicts, our nation sometimes has disputes with other nations. Such disputes can directly threaten our peace and well-being. There are several ways countries try to resolve such conflicts. One approach is diplomacy and negotiation, in which leaders try to compromise: each side to the dispute gives up something to find a middle ground they can all accept. Sometimes, however, American leaders must rely on the use of force and military conflict to resolve disagreements.

Another important way the United States deals with conflicts is by signing international agreements and by participatiing in international organizations. Many of these agreements and organizations seek to promote world trade. By participating in such organizations, American leaders hope to achieve international cooperation, global stability, and world peace. The following is a list of some major international organizations and agreements.

INTERNATIONAL ORGANIZATIONS		
ACRONYM	**ORGANIZATION**	**DESCRIPTION**
EU	European Union	Formerly known as the Common Market or European Economic Community, this association has brought about the free movement of goods and people throughout most of Europe.
GATT*	General Agreement on Tariffs and Trade	This organization of over 100 countries seeks to remove tariff barriers and promote international trade through trade agreements between many countries.
IMF*	International Monetary Fund	This organization provides money to countries in difficulty that are willing to follow IMF recommendations about their economic policies.
NAFTA*	North American Free Trade Agreement	In 1994, Canada, Mexico and the United States created this new trade zone, with the aim of eventually eliminating all tariffs between the three countries.
NATO*	North Atlantic Treaty Organization	This is a military alliance of the United States and Western European nations. A few Eastern European countries, such as Poland, have recently been invited to become members.
OPEC	Organization of Petroleum Exporting Countries	This organization of major oil producing nations seeks to coordinate oil production and set world oil prices.
UN*	United Nations	The UN aims to achieve international peace and security and to promote worldwide cooperation on economic, social, cultural, and humanitarian issues.

** The United States is a member of this organization.*

The hall in which the General Assembly of the United Nations meets, at its headquarters in New York City

SECTION 2 MAJOR CIVICS TERMS AND CONCEPTS

Use the following graphic organizer as a review to see if you can recall these important terms and concepts in civics.

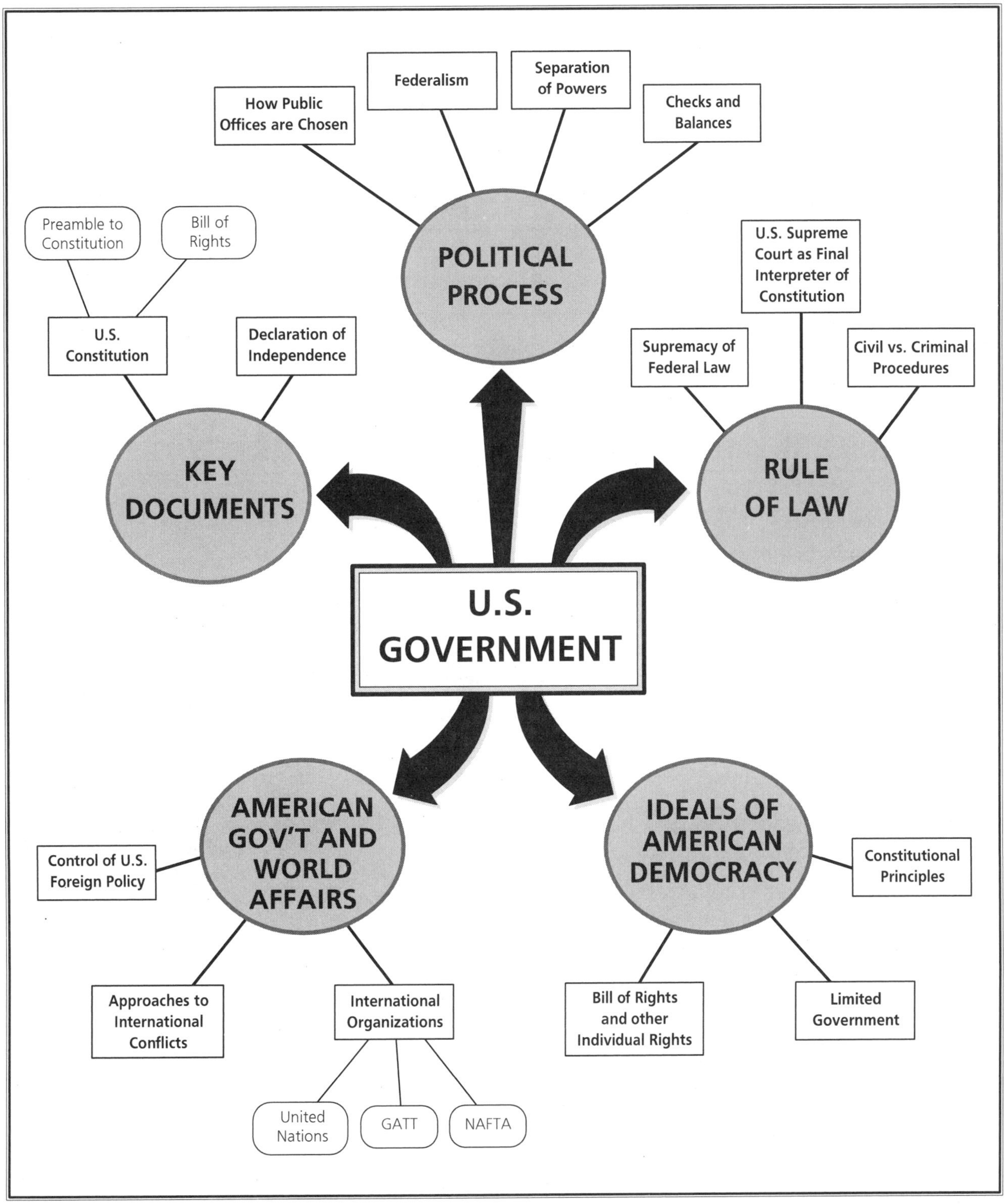

SECTION 3

THE "BIG IDEAS" IN CIVICS

It is important for you to understand the "big ideas" included on the eighth grade MEAP Test in Social Studies. This section explains the "big ideas" for civics, grouped by standard.

STANDARD III.1: PURPOSES OF GOVERNMENT

This standard focuses on the purposes of American government. You should be able to describe how the federal government serves the purposes identified in the Preamble to the Constitution. You should also be able to explain how American citizens benefit from the rule of law, representative democracy, and limited government.

STANDARD III.2: IDEALS OF AMERICAN DEMOCRACY

This standard looks at the Declaration of Independence, the Constitution, and the Bill of Rights. You should be able to identify the basic ideas of the Declaration, such as that the purpose of government is to protect individual rights, and that citizens can overthrow a government that abuses their rights. You should be able to trace the origins of those ideas back to colonial self-government and the English political tradition. You should also be able to explain how the Declaration set a foundation for American political and civic life. Finally, you should be able to explain how the powers of government are limited by the Constitution.

The signing of the Declaration of Independence, 1776

STANDARD III.3: DEMOCRACY IN ACTION

This standard explores the role of law and political activity in American society. It looks at how both legal and political processes help Americans to resolve conflicts and reach

Native Americans being driven from their ancestral lands in the 1800s

decisions. You should be able to distinguish between civil and criminal procedures in our courts. You should also be able to identify disparities between the ideals of American democracy and the realities of American society, and be able to propose ways of bringing our ideals and realities closer together. For example, American ideals promise equality for all, but many groups, such as Native Americans, African Americans, other minority groups, and women have suffered discrimination both in the past and the present.

STANDARD III.4: AMERICAN GOVERNMENT AND POLITICS

This standard focuses on the organization of American government. You should be able to explain how the Constitution operates as the supreme law of the land. You should know how the U.S. Supreme Court interprets the Constitution and strikes down unconstitutional laws. You should also understand the election process and be able to evaluate information from various sources in order to judge candidates for public office.

Members of the U.S. Senate

STANDARD III.5: AMERICAN GOVERNMENT AND WORLD AFFAIRS

This standard examines international relations. You should be able to describe some of the means used by the United States to resolve international conflicts, such as diplomacy, war, and participation in international organizations. In particular, you should be able to describe the functions of major international organizations, such as the United Nations, NATO, and the European Union.

SECTION 4

PRACTICE QUESTIONS

This section contains practice selected-response and constructed-response questions about civics. There are two clusters of selected-response questions, each with a prompt and five questions. Examine each prompt carefully and then answer the questions that follow it. There are also two constructed-response questions, each with a prompt and a writing task. Each question has a benchmark number to indicate which "big idea" is being tested. A detailed list of the civics benchmarks is at the end of this chapter.

— SELECTED-RESPONSE QUESTIONS —

Directions: Read the following passage and use it with what you already know to answer the questions that follow.

"We hold these truths to be self-evident, that all men are created equal, that they are endowed by their Creator with certain unalienable Rights, that among these are Life, Liberty and the pursuit of Happiness. That to secure these rights, Governments are instituted among Men, deriving their just powers from the consent of the governed, That whenever any Form of Government becomes destructive of these ends, it is the right of the People to alter or abolish it, and to institute new Government, laying its foundation on such principles and organizing its powers in such form ..."

1 From which document is this passage taken?

A Articles of Confederation
B Declaration of Independence
C Preamble to the U.S. Constitution
D Bill of Rights

III.2.MS.1

2 Which form of government does this passage support?

A dictatorship
B democracy
C monarchy
D one-party state

III.1.MS.2

3 Which event led to the ideas expressed in this passage?

A The signing of the Mayflower Compact
B The settlement of Jamestown
C The American Revolution
D The purchase of the Louisiana Territory

III.2.MS.1

4 Which belief about the role of government is shared by this passage and the Constitution of the United States?

A The national government is supreme over the state governments.
B Once established, a government's power may not be changed.
C The purpose of government is to serve the needs of its citizens.
D A President can only serve two terms of office.

III.2.MS.2

5 Which other document was written to ensure that the ideas expressed in this document would be carried out?

A The Mayflower Compact
B The Treaty of Paris of 1763
C The Stamp Act
D The Bill of Rights

III.1.MS.4

Name ______________________________ Teacher ______________________________

Directions: Study the following reading passage. Use it with what you already know to answer the questions that follow.

GIDEON V. WAINWRIGHT (1963)

Clarence Gideon was charged with breaking into a pool hall to commit a crime. Too poor to afford a lawyer, Gideon asked the trial judge to appoint an attorney to defend him. The judge turned down his request because Florida law required the appointment of lawyers only in cases where a defendant faced possible execution. Unable to afford a lawyer, Gideon represented himself at the trial. He was found guilty. He appealed his conviction to the Florida Supreme Court, but his appeal was denied.

In jail, Gideon wrote a letter to the U.S. Supreme Court stating that he did not receive a fair trial. The Supreme Court agreed to hear his case. Later, in delivering the majority opinion of the Supreme Court, Justice Hugo Black wrote:

> *"Reason and reflection require us to recognize that in our system of criminal justice, any person [brought] into court, who is too poor to hire a lawyer, cannot be assured a fair trial unless [a lawyer] is provided for him."*

6 Why was this case appealed to the U.S. Supreme Court?

A It involved review of federal law.

B It was first tried in a federal court.

C It involved the State of Florida declaring a federal law unconstitutional.

D It involved the interpretation of a constitutional right.

III.4.MS.2

7 Based on the information in the passage, which statement about the original case is most accurate?

A It was a criminal case heard by a trial court in Florida.

B It was a civil case heard by the U.S. Supreme Court.

C It was a criminal case heard by the U.S. District Court in Washington, D.C.

D It was a civil case heard by the Supreme Court of Florida.

III.3.MS.1

8 If you were the lawyer representing Gideon before the Supreme Court, which quotation would BEST support your case?

A "Congress shall make no law ... prohibiting freedom of speech"

B "In all criminal cases, the accused shall enjoy the right to a speedy and public trial"

C "In all criminal cases, the accused shall ... be confronted with the witnesses against him"

D "In all criminal cases, the accused shall ... have the right to assistance of [a lawyer] for his defense"

III.2.MS.1

9 How might the Supreme Court's ruling in Gideon's case be reversed?

A The President could veto the Supreme Court's decision.

B The Florida legislature could pass a law overturning the decision.

C The Governor of Florida could refuse to obey the Supreme Court's decision.

D The Constitution could be amended to provide that a state must supply a lawyer only in cases involving the death penalty.

III.2.MS.3

10 Justice Hugo Black's opinion, quoted in the passage, is based on the idea that Gideon

A was denied freedom of speech

B was discriminated against by the State of Florida because of his race

C did not receive due process of law

D was innocent and should never have been brought to trial

III.2.MS.1

Name ______________________________ Teacher ______________________________

— CONSTRUCTED-RESPONSE QUESTIONS —

The following section has two constructed-response questions. Read the directions and examine each question carefully before answering.

Directions: You should take about 5 minutes to read the following material and use it with what you already know to complete this task.

Dear Julie,

It was wonderful to hear from you again. I received your letter asking about how the government of the United States is organized. In the United States we have a federal system of government. Our national government and state governments share powers. Let me give you some examples of the powers that the national government and state governments have in order to meet their purposes ....

Your friend,
Matthew

11 On the lines provided, **identify** and **show how** one power of the national government and one power of state government allows that government to meet its purposes.

Identification of one national power: ____

Show how this power allows the national government to meet its purposes: ____

____

____

Identification of one state power: ____

Show how this power allows a state government to meet its purposes: ________

____

____

III.2.MS.3

Name ______________________________ Teacher ______________________________

Directions: You should take about 5 minutes to read the following material and use it with what you already know to complete this task.

The U.S. Constitution sets forth the basic principles upon which our national government was established. The Preamble to our Constitution sets forth the purposes of our national government.

THE PREAMBLE TO THE U.S. CONSTITUTION

We, the people of the United States, in order to form a more perfect Union, establish justice, insure domestic tranquillity [*peace*], provide for the common defense, promote the general welfare, and secure the blessings of liberty to ourselves and our posterity [*future generations*], ... establish this Constitution for the United States of America.

12 On the lines provided, select **one** purpose mentioned in the Preamble and describe how that purpose is carried out by our national government.

Identification of **one** purpose found in the Preamble: ____________________

____

Description of how that purpose is carried out by our national government:

____

____

____

____

____

____

III.1.MS.1

Name ____________________ Teacher ____________________

BENCHMARKS OF THE CIVICS STRAND

Standard III.1: Purposes of Government

III.1.MS.1	Describe how the federal government in the United States serves the purposes set forth in the Preamble to the Constitution.
III.1.MS.2	Distinguish between representative democracy in the United States and other forms of government.
III.1.MS.3	Explain how the rule of law protects individual rights and serves the common good.
III.1.MS.4	Explain the importance of limited government to protect political and economic freedom.

Standard III.2: Ideals of American Democracy

III.2.MS.1	Identify the essential ideas expressed in the Declaration of Independence and the origins of those ideas, and explain how they set the foundation for civic life, politics, and government in the United States.
III.2.MS.2	Explain the means for limiting the powers of government established by the U.S. Constitution.
III.2.MS.3	Describe provisions of the U.S. Constitution which delegate to government the powers necessary to fulfill the purposes for which it was established.

Standard III.3: Democracy In Action

III.3.MS.1	Distinguish between civil and criminal procedure.
III.3.MS.2	Identify disparities between American ideas and realities and propose ways to reduce them.

Standard III.4: American Government and Politics

III.4.MS.1	Evaluate information and arguments from various sources in order to evaluate candidates for public office.
III.4.MS.2	Explain how the Constitution is maintained as the supreme law of the land.

Standard III.5: American Government and World Affairs

III.5.MS.1	Describe the purposes and functions of major international governmental organizations.
III.5.MS.2	Describe means used by the United States to resolve international conflicts.

CHAPTER 10

INQUIRY

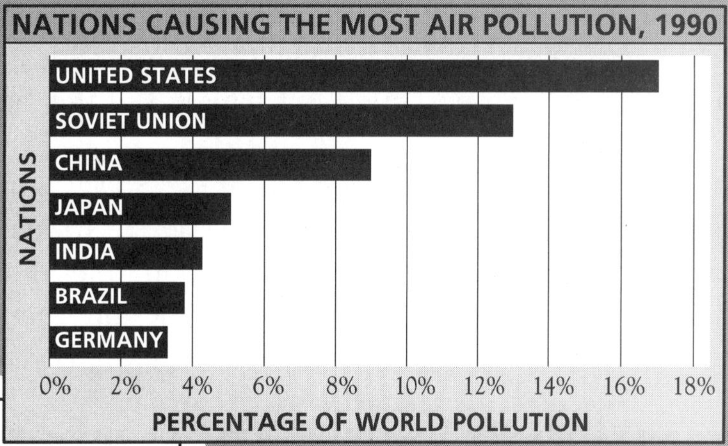

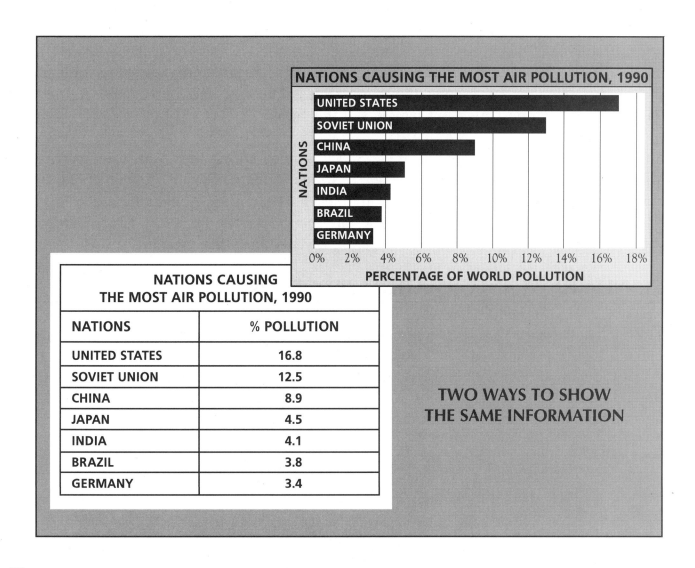

NATIONS CAUSING THE MOST AIR POLLUTION, 1990

NATIONS	% POLLUTION
UNITED STATES	16.8
SOVIET UNION	12.5
CHINA	8.9
JAPAN	4.5
INDIA	4.1
BRAZIL	3.8
GERMANY	3.4

TWO WAYS TO SHOW THE SAME INFORMATION

Section 1: Inquiry Benchmarks

Section 2: Examining an Inquiry Question

Section 3: A Sample Inquiry Question

SECTION 1

INQUIRY BENCHMARKS

One of the main purposes of social studies is to help prepare young people to become responsible citizens. A responsible citizen must be able to participate in making decisions on important issues facing his or her nation, state, and community. In order to participate effectively, a person must be knowledgeable about these issues. In the world today, we often receive information about such issues in a variety of formats, including line graphs, bar graphs, pie charts, tables, timelines, and maps. These formats have already been described in Chapter 3 of this book.

The inquiry section of the eighth grade Social Studies MEAP Test will examine your ability to interpret information from these various formats, as well as your ability to convert information from one format to another. For example, you may be required to interpret a bar graph and to re-format the information it contains into a table. Following is a description of the "big ideas" that will be tested for this standard.

STANDARD V.1: INFORMATION PROCESSING

This standard focuses on the means of acquiring information for informed decision-making as a responsible citizen. You should be able to locate and interpret information about the natural environments and cultures of other countries using primary and secondary sources, social science information, and electronic technologies. You should also be able to organize this information into maps, graphs, and tables.

Now that you are familiar with what the inquiry strand focuses on, let's look at a typical inquiry question:

SECTION 2

EXAMINING AN INQUIRY QUESTION

Directions: You should take about five minutes to study the following material and use it with what you already know to complete these tasks.

A modern economy requires a highly educated workforce to be productive. Listed below are several countries and their various literacy rates — the percentage of adults who are able to read and write — as well as each country's per capita *(per person)* Gross Domestic Product.

WORLD LITERACY RATES

COUNTRY	LITERACY RATE	PER CAPITA GDP (in US Dollars)
Bangladesh	35%	$240
Germany	100%	$27,510
Haiti	45%	$870
Japan	100%	$39,640
Mali	31%	$250
United States	96%	$26,980

Task I

1 Study the information in the graph. Make a statement about the *relationship* between **literacy rates** and **per capita Gross Domestic Product**.

____

____

____

____

V.1.MS.1

continued ...

TASK II

2 Use the information in the table to make a bar graph showing the gross domestic product per capita of these countries. In addition, title it and correctly label each axis.

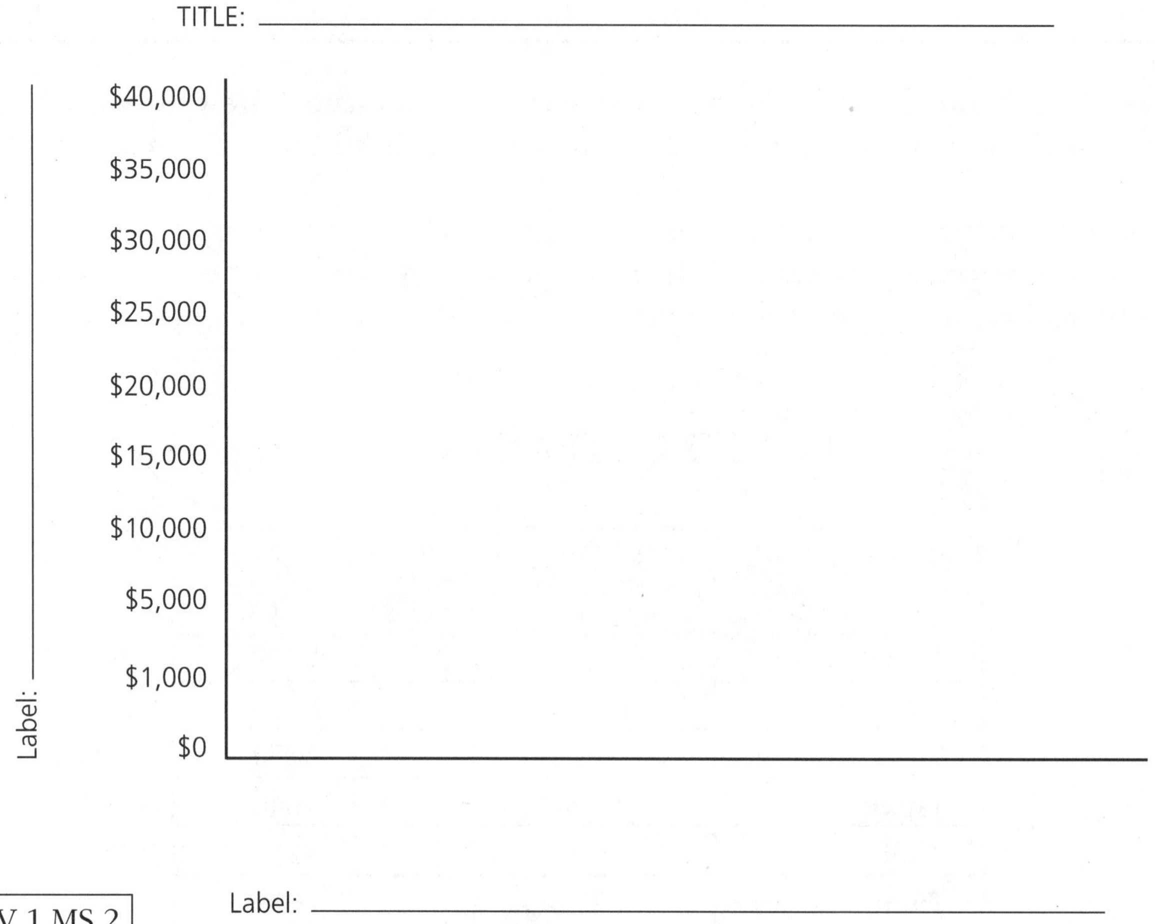

V.1.MS.2

A careful examination of the question shows that there are three parts for you to deal with:

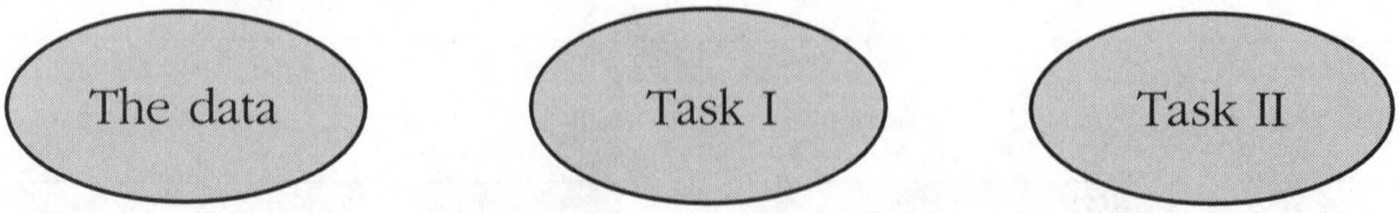

Let's look at each part separately, to see what is required in presenting an answer.

THE DATA: An inquiry question will always present you with some information, usually about a general topic. In the data presented, there will be **two** things

Name________________________________ Teacher____________________________________

(called *variables*) that deal with the general topic. In our sample question, the general topic and the two variables are as follows:

General Topic:	World literacy rates
Variable #1:	Literacy rates
Variable #2:	Per capita Gross Domestic Product

TASK I: In Task I, you are asked to make a **connection** or to identify a **relationship** between the two variables by answering a selected-response question. The question is testing your ability to see common patterns. You have to look at the specific information with the purpose of finding a common pattern, general connection, or generalization. A **generalization** is a general statement that identifies a common pattern among several different facts.

In the table on page 125, you can see that countries with the highest literacy rates (Japan, Germany, and the United States), also have the highest per capita GDP. On the other hand, countries with the lowest literacy rates, (Haiti, Mali and Bangladesh) have the lowest per capita GDP. This question tests your ability to interpret social science information about the cultures of other regions using a primary source.

TASK II: In Task II, you will always be asked to take the information in the data and to **reorganize** it into **another type of data format**. For example, you may be given map information and be asked to put it into a table format. What Task II really tests is your knowledge of data formats *(prompts)*. You have to know how the different formats are constructed. Chapter 3, you will recall, has a detailed description of each type of format.

In our sample question, you had to take information from a table format and transform it into a bar graph. In order to do this, you had to know the meaning of the horizontal and vertical axis on a graph. Such questions test your ability to organize social science information into maps, graphs, and tables.

On the following page is a model answer to Task II.

PER CAPITA GDP OF SELECTED COUNTRIES

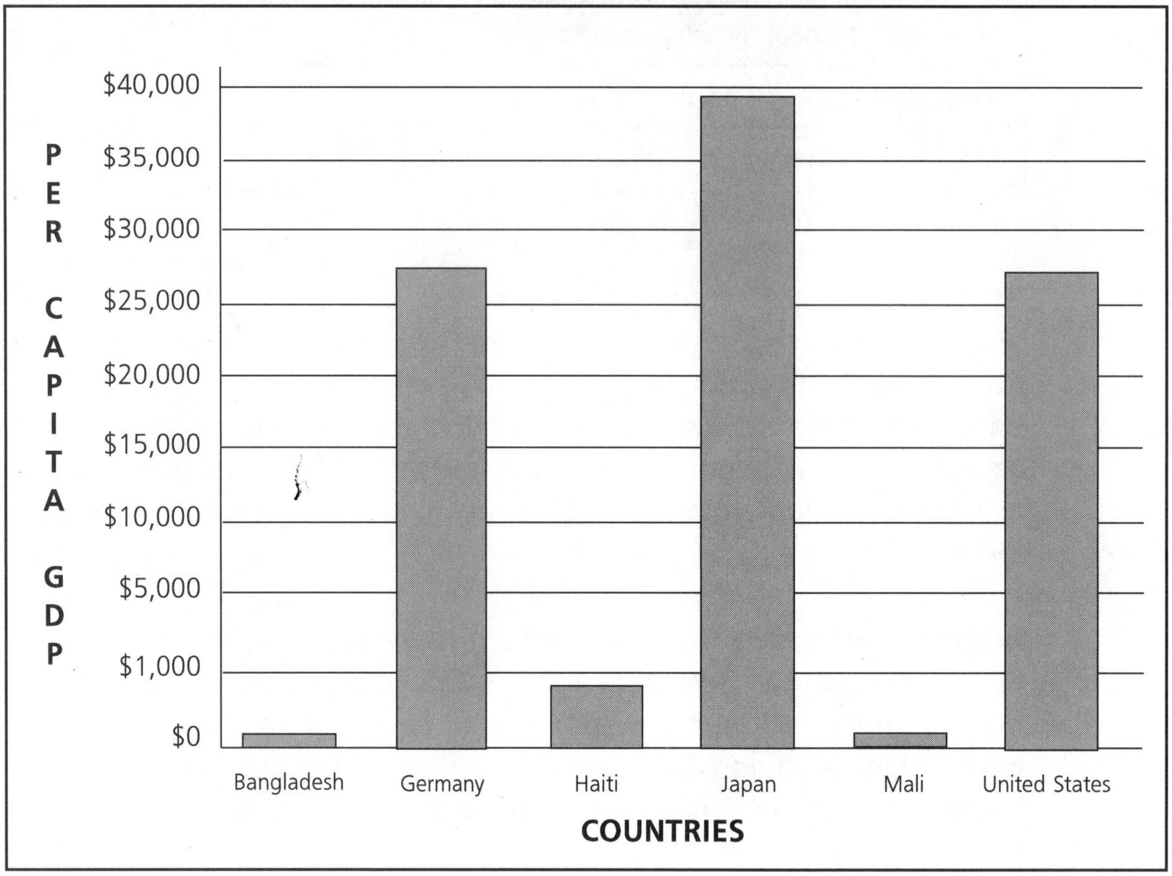

SECTION 3

A SAMPLE INQUIRY QUESTION

Let's test your understanding of inquiry questions. Answer the following sample question.

Directions: You should take about five minutes to study the following material and use it with what you already know to complete these tasks.

The world's population is increasing at a rapid rate. It is estimated that by the year 2025 the population of the world will be about 8 billion people.

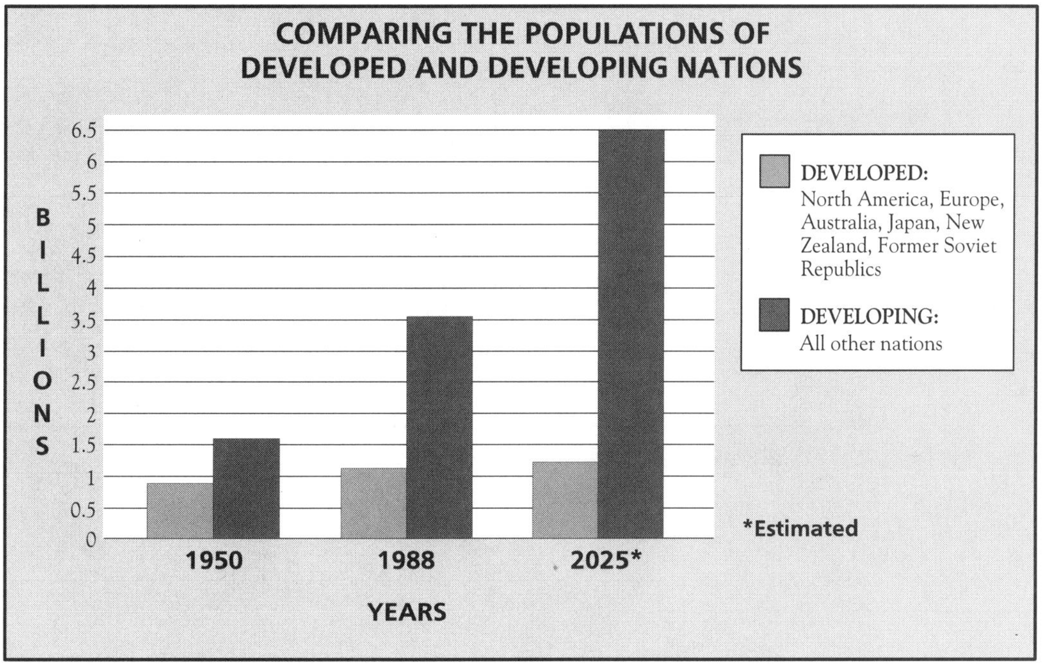

TASK I

1 Study the information in the bar graph. Make a statement about the *relationship* between the **population of developed nations** and the **population of developing nations**.

____

____

____ V.1.MS.3

Name__________________________ Teacher__________________________

TASK II

2 Use the information in the bar graph on page 129 to make a line graph comparing the populations of developed and developing nations. In addition, give the graph a title, correctly label each axis, and complete the key.

TITLE: ____

Label: ____________________

Label: ____

V.1.MS2

KEY

——— =

– – – =

Name____________________________ Teacher______________________________

CHAPTER 11

PUBLIC DISCOURSE AND DECISION-MAKING: ANSWERING EXTENDED-RESPONSE QUESTIONS

Local petition drive

Protesters on the steps of the U.S. Capitol Building

Members of the Michigan Militia

Section 1: Extended-Response Questions

Section 2: The Core Democratic Values

Section 3: A Sample Extended-Response Question

SECTION 1 EXTENDED-RESPONSE QUESTIONS

The last type of question on the Social Studies MEAP Test is known as an **extended-response question**. These questions ask you to write a short essay or letter about a **public policy issue**. There will be two of these on the test. This chapter will show you how to answer an extended-response question, in three steps:

- ✦ First, you will learn what a "public policy issue" is;
- ✦ Second, you will identify *core democratic values*; and
- ✦ Third, you will analyze a public policy issue and examine a sample extended-response question.

DEFINING A "PUBLIC POLICY" ISSUE

An **issue** is a topic about which people have different points of view. A **public policy issue** is an issue of concern to an entire community. The community could be your town, state, or the entire nation. Public policy issues often center on whether the government should pass a law or take some other action to resolve a problem. Public policy issues are often stated as "should" questions:

- ✦ *Should* the community ban the use of skateboards on public property?
- ✦ *Should* Congress make it illegal to import products made by child labor?
- ✦ *Should* Congress limit the violence shown on television?

There is NO "right" or "wrong" side to an issue. People will take different positions based on their points of view. When asked to state your position on an issue, you should present the opinion you think is best. Then you *must* support your position with reasons and facts.

SECTION 2 THE CORE DEMOCRATIC VALUES

In making decisions about public issues, Americans apply a set of common values. A **value** is something we consider important and worthwhile. We refer to the values of American society as the **core democratic values**.

The idea that every person has worth and dignity is one of the most basic of our core democratic values. American society is based on the principle that the importance of every person should be recognized and respected by others.

Our core democratic values are found mainly in two key documents from our history: the **Declaration of Independence** and the **U.S. Constitution**. These documents can be thought of as two mighty pillars supporting our society.

The first public reading of the Declaration of Independence in Philadelphia, July 8, 1776

In the Declaration of Independence, Americans declared their freedom from Great Britain. The Declaration also announced that there were certain basic truths about people that all governments should recognize. One of these truths was that the purpose of government should be to protect the "life, liberty and pursuit of happiness" of its citizens.

As you know, the U.S. Constitution later established the basic system of American government. It also guaranteed certain rights to all Americans. A **right** is the freedom to do (or *not* to do) something. Our most important constitutional rights are found in five areas:

- **Individual Rights**
- **Equality**
- **Justice**
- **Representative Government**
- **The Common Good**

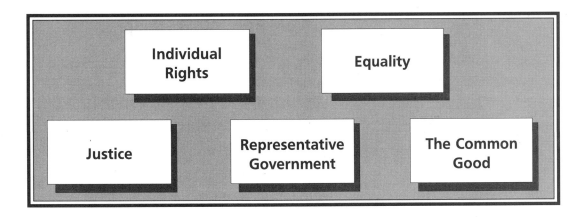

On the following page is a chart listing core democratic values that may appear on the Social Studies MEAP Test. In each extended-response question, you will be asked to refer to at least one of these core democratic values and to explain how it supports your position.

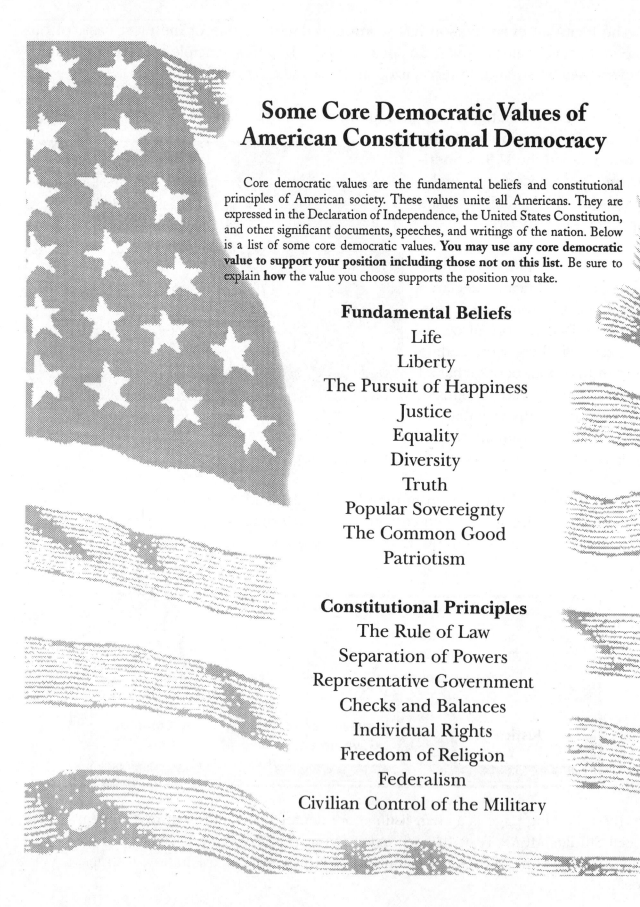

Some Core Democratic Values of American Constitutional Democracy

Core democratic values are the fundamental beliefs and constitutional principles of American society. These values unite all Americans. They are expressed in the Declaration of Independence, the United States Constitution, and other significant documents, speeches, and writings of the nation. Below is a list of some core democratic values. **You may use any core democratic value to support your position including those not on this list.** Be sure to explain **how** the value you choose supports the position you take.

Fundamental Beliefs

Life
Liberty
The Pursuit of Happiness
Justice
Equality
Diversity
Truth
Popular Sovereignty
The Common Good
Patriotism

Constitutional Principles

The Rule of Law
Separation of Powers
Representative Government
Checks and Balances
Individual Rights
Freedom of Religion
Federalism
Civilian Control of the Military

INDIVIDUAL RIGHTS

Our tradition of individual rights began in the 1600s when the first English settlers came to North America. As subjects of the British monarchy, which had an official state religion, many colonists left England in search of a place where they could practice their own religion freely. People of several different religious beliefs soon settled in the American colonies. Eventually, the colonists decided that everyone should be free to practice his or her own religion.

Other new rights emerged under colonial conditions in America. After the United States became an independent country, these rights were guaranteed by the first ten amendments to the Constitution, known as the **Bill of Rights**. The rights listed below are those guaranteed by the First Amendment.

Freedom of the Press. People have the right to print their ideas and beliefs even if they criticize the government.

Freedom of Speech. People have the right to express their ideas and beliefs in public.

Freedom of Assembly. People have the right to hold public meetings, even if their purpose is to protest government actions.

Freedom to Petition Government. People have the right to write to government leaders and ask them to make changes.

EQUALITY

American society is based on the cooperation of many different groups. We all expect to be treated fairly by our government and by our fellow citizens. Because of our belief in equality, everyone — regardless of race, ethnic background, or gender — is guaranteed "equal protection" under the law. This means that the government cannot pass laws that unfairly favor some groups while harming others.

JUSTICE

Americans believe that justice must be administered fairly, as expressed in the phrase "due process of law." This means the government must follow specific procedures when it accuses someone of a crime or wants to take away someone's property for the public good. For example, people accused of a crime must be tried by a jury of fellow citizens, according to established rules. They also have the right *not* to testify at their own trial. The following graphic organizer will help you to remember some of the most important rights of individuals accused of a crime:

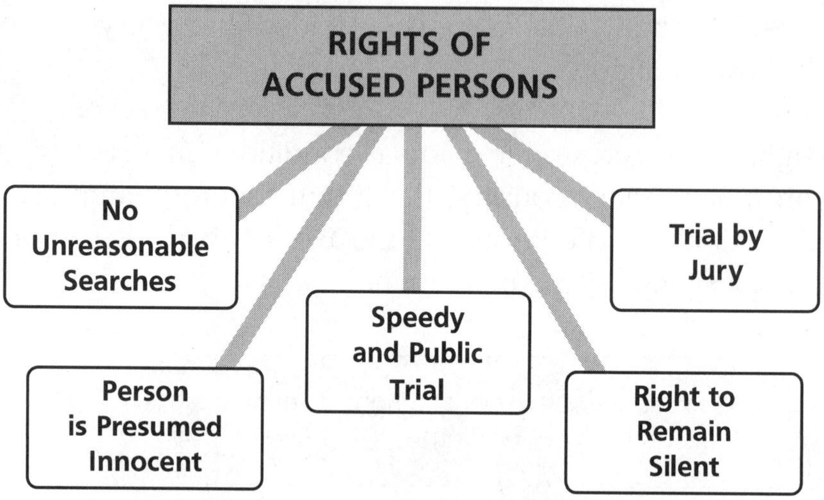

It is useful to remember that the protection of the rights of accused people sends a powerful message throughout society. Individual rights are important and must be respected. Our laws attempt to make sure that the government cannot punish people for crimes they did not commit. Each of us feels safer because we know that we cannot be arrested or punished without due process of law.

REPRESENTATIVE GOVERNMENT

Our beliefs in **popular sovereignty** *(rule by the people)* and **representative government** form another part of our core democratic values. Americans believe that government should serve the interests of the people. Voters elect representatives to run the government and to carry out the will of the citizens.

THE COMMON GOOD

Although Americans prize individual freedom, they also value the community. It is only by acting together that Americans can develop resources, increase knowledge, run a modern economy, and defend their country. For this reason, promoting the **common good** — the well-being of the entire community — is another core democratic value. Sometimes a public issue arises when promoting the common good would mean restricting some individual rights.

SECTION 3 — A SAMPLE EXTENDED-RESPONSE QUESTION

This sample question is similar to the extended-response questions on the MEAP Test.

Directions: Read the following information about an imaginary public policy issue. Use it with what you already know to complete the tasks that follow. You should take about 20 minutes to complete both Task I and Task II. Task I is a selected-response item and Task II is an extended-response item.

A HIGH-SPEED RAILWAY

The states of Michigan and Illinois have decided to build a high-speed railway connecting the cities of Detroit and Chicago. Each state will pay for half of the construction costs with money collected from state taxpayers. Although the project will cost billions of dollars, it will reduce traffic congestion between the two cities. Some experts believe it will also encourage economic growth.

DATA SECTION

PART A The following shows the results of a public opinion survey of residents in Michigan and Illinois, taken by a Detroit television news station.

RESULTS OF THE TELEVISION STATION SURVEY

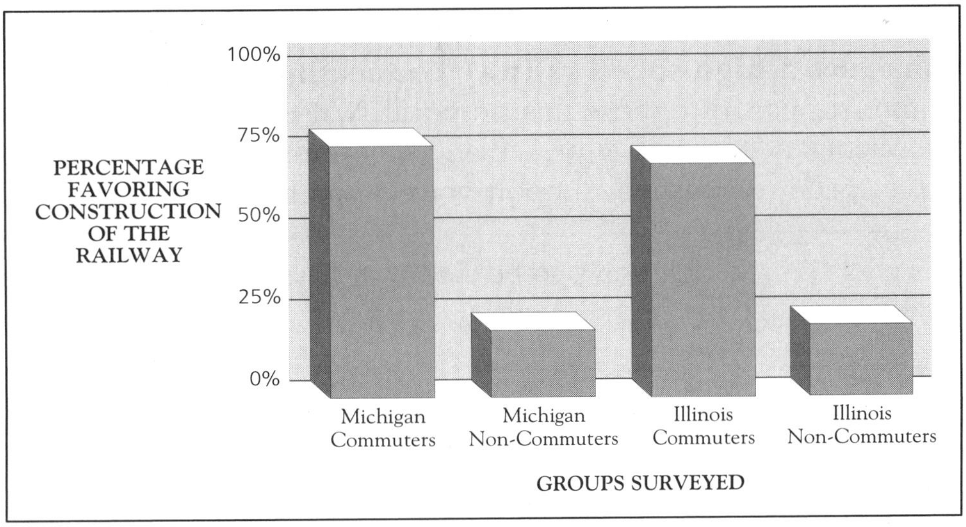

(continued...)

PART B A study was conducted by a joint state commission. The following graph provides some projections by experts of the costs of the railway link, and its possible impact on the economy of Michigan and Illinois.

RESULTS OF THE JOINT STATE COMMISSION STUDY

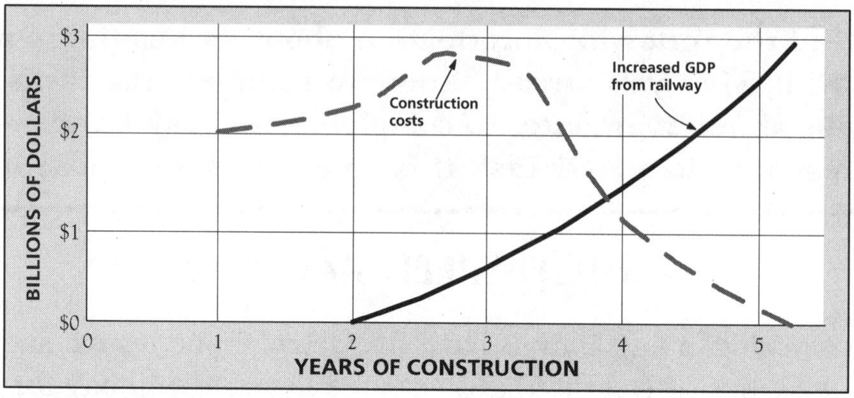

COMPLETE THE FOLLOWING TASKS:

Task I: Interpreting Information

Study the information in the Data Section. Which of the following statements best describes the *relationship* between **commuting** and **a person's opinion about the proposed railway**? Be sure to mark your answer on the answer sheet.

A Illinois commuters favor construction more strongly than Michigan commuters.
B Whether a person commutes has no effect on that person's opinion.
C Commuters are more likely to favor construction than non-commuters.
D Non-commuters favor construction more than commuters.

Task II: Taking A Stand

You will now take a stand on the following public issue: **Should Michigan and Illinois construct a high-speed railway connecting Detroit and Chicago?** You may either support or oppose this proposal. Write a letter to your representative in the Michigan House of Representatives expressing your opinion. Use information to provide reasons that support your position.

You will be graded on the following, so be sure your letter includes each of the elements listed below:

- A clear statement of your position.
- Supporting information using core democratic values of American constitutional democracy. (See page 134 for examples.)
- Supporting knowledge from history, geography, civics, or economics that you already know. (It is not enough to state only your opinion.)
- Supporting information from the Data Section.

continued...

Remember to: Use complete sentences.
Explain your reasons in detail.
Write or print neatly on the lines provided.

Should Michigan and Illinois build a high-speed railway connecting Detroit and Chicago?

Dear Representative:

continued...

Use this checklist to review your letter:

- ❑ I stated my position clearly.
- ❑ I supported my position with reference to at least one core democratic value of American constitutional democracy.
- ❑ I supported my position with knowledge from history, geography, civics, or economics that I already knew.
- ❑ I supported my position with information from the Data Section.

As you can see from this sample, extended-response questions consist of two main parts: Task I and Task II. Let's take a closer look at each of these.

ANSWERING THE QUESTION: TASK I

Task I tests your understanding of information in the Data Section. As explained in the previous chapter on inquiry, Task I asks you to make a **connection** or to find a **relationship** between two variables (whether a person commutes and opinions about building the railway). This part of the task tests your ability to see common patterns in specific examples. Let's focus on the two pieces of evidence in the Data Section.

Part A contains a bar graph showing how commuters and non-commuters from each state feel about the proposed railway. Task I in this question asks you to interpret the data in Part A. Look at the specific groups listed in the bar graph in Part A. You should notice that commuters (people who travel to work) generally favor the train more than people who do not commute. The correct answer for Task I is choice **C**. All the other statements are incorrect, according to the bar graph.

Part B contains a table showing what experts believe the railway will cost to build each year, and how it will increase the GDP of Michigan and Illinois. For example, in the first year construction costs will be $2 billion. They will rise the next year to $2.8 billion. After that, they will drop until the railway is completed in the fifth year.

ANSWERING THE QUESTION: TASK II

Task II asks you to take a stand on a public policy issue by expressing your opinion in writing. In your written answer, you must:

- base your opinion on one of the core democratic values;
- support your position with information from the Data Section; and
- support your answer with information from your knowledge of social studies.

USING THE 5-S APPROACH

Before you begin Task II of an extended-response question, you should take a few minutes to jot down some notes to help you write your answer. One simple way to remember what to do is think of the **5 S's**:

State your position.

Select a Core Democratic Value to support your opinion.

Support your position with evidence from the Data Section.

Support your position with evidence from your social studies knowledge.

Summarize your argument.

Let's see how using this method can bring all of these factors together into a logical, well-organized letter.

PRE-WRITING NOTES

State your Position

After reading the question and analyzing the Data Section, you should form your own opinion. In our sample question, that means you would either support or oppose the construction of the high-speed railway.

Select a Core Democratic Value

Your position must be supported by a core democratic value. Although a long list of core democratic values exists (see. p. 134), most issues will focus on five main values.

1. **INDIVIDUAL RIGHTS/LIBERTY.** Many of these rights, such as free speech and freedom of religion, are guaranteed in the Bill of Rights. If the question deals with limiting the freedom of individuals, you can refer to this core democratic value. Here, if you oppose the project, you could state that property-owners in the way of the railroad would have to give up their property.

2. **EQUALITY.** The 14th Amendment to the Constitution states that all Americans must be treated fairly and equally under the law. If the question deals with treating some groups differently than others, you might refer to this core democratic value. Here, if you oppose the project, you might state that commuters would be getting special treatment if the railway was built.

(continued...)

3. JUSTICE. Americans are very concerned with protecting their liberties and property from unfair acts by government. If the question deals with taking away the property or rights of a person or group, then the core democratic value of justice may be involved. Here, you might say that it is unjust to build the railway without having a public hearing in which people who oppose the project can express their views. You might also say it is unfair to use taxpayers' money to build a railway that only benefits some groups and not all.

4. REPRESENTATIVE GOVERNMENT. The United States has a representative government. This means the government usually does what the majority of people, who elect government officials, want to do. If you decided to support building the railway, you could refer to this core democratic value, because one of the pieces of data in the Data Section shows that a large number of people in both states support it. However, we don't know if this is a majority of citizens.

5. THE COMMON GOOD. Our democratic society tries to do what is best for the community. Therefore, if the question deals with something that you think would benefit the community, support your position with this core democratic value. Here, you could say that the proposed railway would reduce traffic congestion and pollution and promote economic growth. Or, if you oppose the railway, you could say that the common good sometimes comes into conflict with another core democratic value — individual rights — and you believe individual rights, the right to keep one's money, are more important in this case.

Support Your Position with Evidence from the Data Section

Return to the Data Section. Look for information to use that supports your point of view. For example, in this case the majority of commuters favored construction of the railway. On the other hand, the data also show that non-commuters would have to pay a large amount of taxes to build a railway they probably do not use.

Support Your Position with Your Social Studies Knowledge

To support your position using your social studies knowledge, you should keep in mind some of the basic concepts of geography, history, economics, and civics. For example:

Geography. Look at the situation in the question. Are any of the five themes of geography involved? If so, identify which ones. For example, we know that people are influenced by their environment. You might mention that the railway would reduce traffic and air pollution. Or you might point out that both

(continued...)

Detroit and Chicago are important urban centers. Making it easier to get from one city to the other would encourage trade and economic growth.

History. Again, look at the question. Have you ever studied a past situation similar to the public issue described in the question? It is especially relevant to draw on your history knowledge when two sides are opposed to each other. You might refer to groups that once opposed each other and then resolved their conflict through compromise — as Michigan and Ohio did over the Toledo Strip. Here, you might point out that improvements in transportation such as the Erie Canal and the transcontinental railroad have usually led to big increases in economic growth.

Economics. Again, think carefully about the issue presented in the question. If it involves spending government money, think about how the government will raise the money — probably through taxes. You might also refer to the idea of "opportunity cost," since every decision to buy something involves opportunity costs. If the government spends money to solve the problem in the question, what other problems might go unsolved for lack of money? In our sample question, Michigan and Illinois would spend billions of dollars to build the railway. Could this money be used in a better way?

Civics. As always, start by looking at the public policy issue in the question and the evidence in the Data Section. Will the local, state, or national government be involved? If so, mention what powers or roles the government will play in addressing the issue. Would government be going beyond its constitutional powers by adopting the project suggested in the question? In our sample question, it is helpful to recall that one of the main roles of state government is to promote the public good.

Summarize your Argument

At the end of your response, you should again state your position on the issue. This should be done in an affirmative way (not saying what you are *against,* but what you are *in favor of*). For example:

"As a result of the arguments I have presented in this letter,
I feel that Michigan and Illinois should build the high-speed railway."

WRITING YOUR LETTER OR ESSAY

The last step is to convert your pre-writing notes into a letter (or essay, depending on which type of writing the question asks for). As you write, remember to follow the same **5-S** approach you just read about.

Dear Representative:

I believe a high-speed railway should be built between the cities of Detroit and Chicago. I feel this way for a number of reasons.

State your position

One of the most important core democratic values is the common good. This means our government should take actions that will benefit the entire community. Building a high-speed railway will benefit citizens of both Michigan and Illinois, as the rest of this letter will show.

Select a core democratic value to support your position

My opinion is further supported by the projections of experts shown in the Data Section. These experts predict that completing the railway will have a positive impact on the Gross Domestic Product of Michigan and Illinois. By the time the railway is complete, in the fifth year, Michigan and Illinois will have an increase in GDP of more than $2 billion per year.

Select supporting evidence from the Data Section

We know from history that improvements in transportation often lead to big increases in economic growth. For example, the completion of the Erie Canal made it possible to ship goods from the Great Lakes down to New York City. Even though the Erie Canal was expensive to build, it paid for itself over time. The canal made New York City a major port and contributed to the growth of Michigan. The same beneficial results can be projected for the proposed high-speed railway.

Select supporting evidence from your social studies knowledge

In conclusion, I would like you to vote for the railway because it will reduce congestion and pollution and favor economic growth in our state. This promotes the public good of all citizens. As a result of the arguments I have presented in this letter, I feel Michigan and Illinois should build the high-speed railway.

Summarize your positon

Sincerely yours,

____

(Sign your name)

REMEMBER: Use this basic framework in writing your answer to **any** extended-response question.

CHAPTER 12

A PRACTICE MEAP TEST IN SOCIAL STUDIES

You have now reviewed what you need to know to do well on the 8th grade Social Studies MEAP Test. At this point, you are ready to take a practice test.

You should take the following test under "test conditions." This means taking the entire test in a quiet room. Complete the test in two separate sessions, as indicated. This will give you a feeling for what the actual test will be like. Taking this practice test will reduce any anxiety you might have about the real test.

The practice test will also help you to identify areas that you still need to study and review. For example, after taking the test you may find you had problems answering selected-response questions on history or extended-response questions on public policy issues. In that case, you should review the sections of this book focusing on those types of questions.

Good luck on this practice test!

DAY ONE: SOCIAL STUDIES ASSESSMENT

Instructions to the Student

There are three types of questions on this test: **selected-response, constructed-response**, and **extended-response**.

- **Selected-response** questions will ask you first to read a passage, map, chart, or table. After studying this prompt, read the questions and choose the best answer from among four answer choices.

- **Constructed-response** questions will ask you to explain a conclusion, provide examples, complete a chart, interpret information, or give a reason for an answer you have given.

- **Extended-response** questions require you to write an answer that is more detailed and requires more thinking. These items ask you to interpret information from a set of data on an imaginary policy issue, identify a relationship presented in the Data Section, take a position for or against the policy, and give reasons supporting your position.

Use the separate answer sheet (see page 181) to mark your choices for the **selected-response** questions. Fill in the circle for your choice on the answer sheet. Remember to fill in the circle completely and cleanly, erasing any stray lines or marks.

Space is provided in the test section for you to write your answers to **constructed-response** and **extended-response** items.

Read all directions for these items carefully.

If you finish early, you may check your work for Day One **only**. Do **not** go ahead and work on the Day Two section of this test.

Geography

Directions: Study the following map and use it with what you already know to answer the questions that follow.

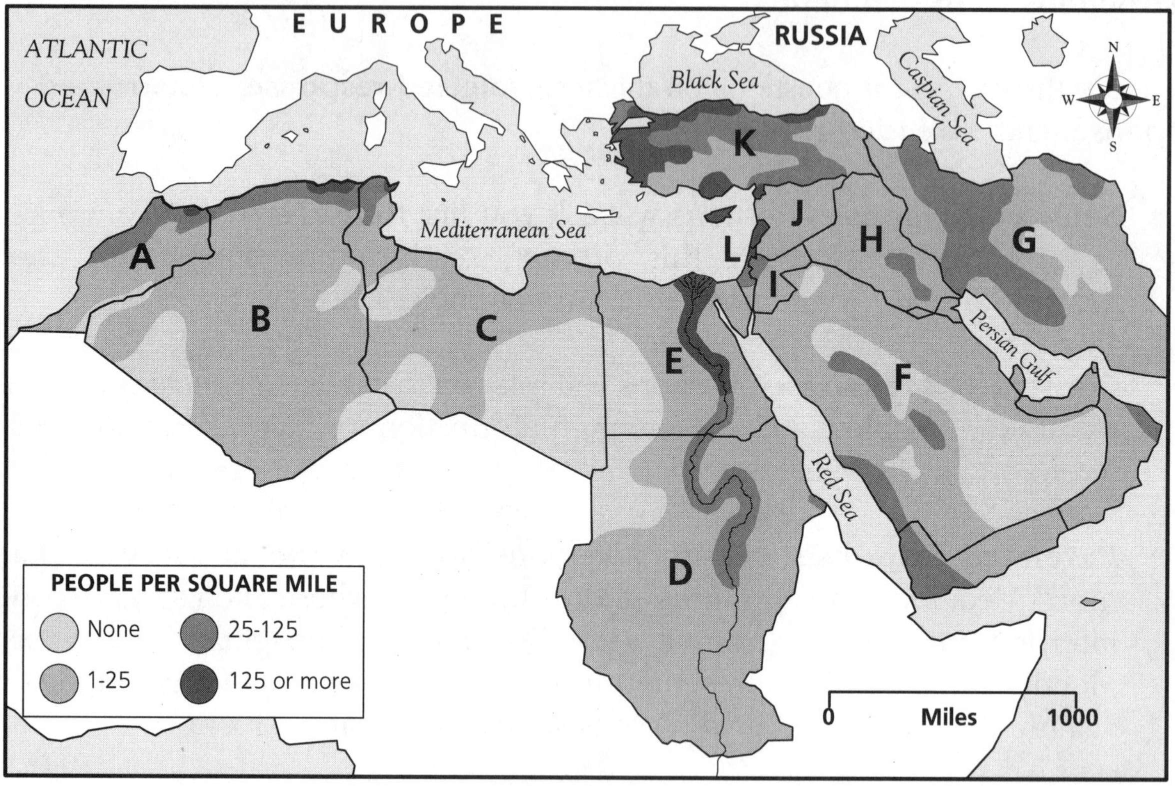

Geography

1 On which continent are Countries A, B, C and D located?

A Africa
B Europe
C Asia
D South America

II.4.MS.4

2 Which title would be MOST appropriate for the map?

A Major Waterways of Europe
B Population Distribution of North Africa and the Middle East
C Population of North Africa
D Physical Features of the Middle East

II.4.MS.3

3 Which topographic factor BEST explains why large parts of Country B, Country C, and Country E are uninhabited?

A These areas lie in the Sahara Desert.
B These areas have some of the world's highest mountain ranges.
C These areas are mostly covered by jungles.
D These areas lie in a tropical rain forest.

II.2.MS.3

4 Which statement BEST explains the distribution of population shown on the map?

A Areas near waterways tend to have high population densities.
B Most of these areas are located close to Russia.
C Areas near waterways tend to have low population densities.
D People are attracted to warm climates.

II.2.MS.5

5 What characteristic is shared by most people living in the countries shown on the map?

A A majority of their citizens follow the Islamic religion.
B English is their official language.
C They are ruled by hereditary kings.
D They border the Suez Canal.

II.1.MS.2

Geography

Directions: Look at the following photographs and use them with what you already know to answer the questions that follow.

Photograph 1

Photograph 5

Photograph 2

Photograph 6

Photograph 3

Photograph 7

Photograph 4

Photograph 8

Geography

6 Which title would be MOST appropriate for this collection of photographs?

A Capitals of the World
B Historic World Places
C Cities of Europe and Asia
D Pre-Columbian Achievements

II.1.MS.1

7 You are planning a summer vacation to the landmarks shown in Photographs 5 and 7. Which area of the world would you be traveling to?

A Middle East
B Latin America
C Sub-Saharan Africa
D Europe

II.4.MS.4

8 Assume a dispute arose between two nations. Which photograph depicts a place where the two nations might come to work out their differences?

A Photograph 2
B Photograph 4
C Photograph 6
D Photograph 8

II.3.MS.4

9 The institution shown in Photograph 3 is important to the United States because

A it is the religious center for many Arab Americans
B it serves as the headquarters of the United Nations
C America's democratic system owes part of its origins to that institution
D it is a former colonial possession of the United States

II.3.MS.4

10 Which pair of photographs show one location that used to have a Communist form of government and a second location still under Communist rule?

A Photographs 4 and 6
B Photographs 1 and 6
C Photographs 1 and 4
D Photographs 7 and 8

II.4.MS.4

Name ______________________ Teacher ______________________

Geography

Directions: You should take about 5 minutes to read the following advertisement and use it with what you already know to complete this task.

The following advertisement recently appeared in several newspapers throughout Michigan.

ATTENTION STUDENTS!

TRAVEL WILL BE AVAILABLE THIS SUMMER TO THE FOLLOWING LOCATIONS:

Trip 1: Libya's Sahara Desert
Trip 2: Thailand's Rain Forest
Trip 3: Russia's Tundra
Trip 4: Peru's Andes Mountains

Geography

11 On the lines provided, describe the characteristics of **two** of the locations mentioned in the advertisement.

Identification of one area and its characteristics:

____

____

____

____

Identification of a second area and its characteristics:

____

____

____

____

II.2.MS.1

Name ____________________________ Teacher ____________________________

History

Directions: Examine the following timeline and use it with what you already know to answer the questions that follow.

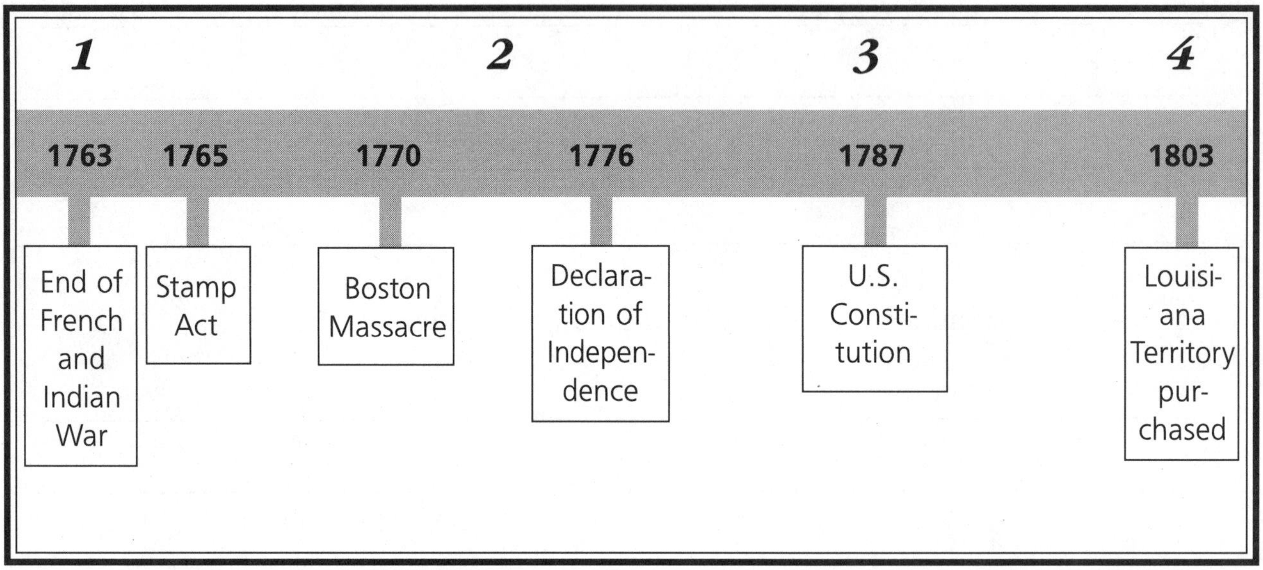

12 The events in the timeline span which TWO centuries?

A 15th and 16th
B 16th and 17th
C 17th and 18th
D 18th and 19th

I.2.MS.1

13 Which title BEST descibes the events shown on the timeline?

A Colonization and Settlement
B Revolution and the New Nation
C Expansion and Reform
D Civil War and Reconstruction

I.1.MS.2

14 At what point on the timeline would you place the event known as the "Boston Tea Party?"

A Point 1
B Point 2
C Point 3
D Point 4

I.1.MS.1

15 Which person's achievements might find a place on this timeline?

A Christopher Columbus
B Benjamin Franklin
C William Penn
D Lord Baltimore

I.2.MS.3

16 Which event came after the period covered by this timeline?

A The British set fire to Washington, D.C.
B The Articles of Confederation were approved
C George Washington was elected first U.S. President
D Fighting broke out at Lexington and Concord

I.1.MS.1

History

Directions: Read the following passage and use it with what you already know to answer the questions that follow.

CRISPUS ATTUCKS
(1723-1770)

Historians know very little about the life of Crispus Attucks before the evening of March 5, 1770. It is believed that Attucks, formerly an enslaved African, worked as a seaman on the Boston docks. After eating dinner at a nearby inn, Attucks joined a crowd of people watching a demonstration taking place on King Street.

A group of young boys were demonstrating against British rule in the colonies. The boys were throwing snowballs and sticks at a British sentry near the Boston Customhouse. As tensions mounted, a nearby squad of British soldiers arrived to aid the sentry. The soldiers pushed against the crowd with their guns. Attucks, a stout man with a long stick, threw himself into the battle. He swung at one of the soldiers, knocking away the soldier's gun and striking him on the head.

Captain Thomas Preston, the British officer in charge, cried "Fire!" His soldiers fired into the crowd. Attucks and two other demonstrators were killed immediately. Soon after, Captain Preston and eight of his men were arrested for manslaughter. At their trial, two soldiers were convicted and given light punishments. Preston and six of his soldiers were acquitted.

News of the incident sent shock waves throughout the colonies. Attucks was the first American to die in the coming struggle for independence — a martyr in the name of liberty. He became a symbol of American opposition to the harsh rule imposed by the British in the colonies.

History

17 Which of the following would be a SECONDARY SOURCE for finding out more about the central figure in the reading passage?

A a diary entry by Captain Preston describing that day
B notes by Preston's lawyer about arguments to be used in the trial
C a book by an American historian about Crispus Attucks
D court testimony by a British soldier who fired at the crowd

I.3.MS.1

18 Which core democratic value motivated the actions of Attucks in this passage?

A Separation of Powers
B Freedom of Religion
C Federalism
D Liberty

I.4.MS.4

19 Which of the following events in U.S. history took place shortly after the events described in this passage?

A landing of the first settlers at Jamestown, Virginia
B start of the American Revolution
C start of the War of 1812
D outbreak of the Civil War

I.1.MS.2

20 The shooting described in the narrative was a major event eventually leading to the

A Declaration of Independence
B Mayflower Compact
C Gettysburg Address
D Magna Carta

I.2.MS.1

21 Which event in American history was MOST similar to the events portrayed in the passage?

A Native Americans joining with the French against British rule
B delegates meeting in Philadelphia at the First Continental Congress
C colonists protesting British rule by dumping tea into Boston Harbor
D the British Parliament passing the Stamp Act

I.2.MS.1

History

Directions: You should take about 5 minutes to read the following sign and use it with what you already know to complete this task.

The following appeared throughout the United States in 1786.

ATTENTION STATE LEADERS

OUR COUNTRY FACES MANY PROBLEMS.

A MEETING SHALL BE HELD

IN PHILADELPHIA

IN MAY OF 1787

TO RESOLVE THEM.

History

22 On the lines provided, identify **one** problem hinted at in the sign and discuss how it was resolved at the meeting in Philadelphia.

Identification of one problem hinted at in the sign: ______________________________

____

____

____

____

____

____

____

Explanation of how it was resolved: ______________________________

____

____

____

____

____

____

____

I.1.MS.2

Name ______________________________ Teacher ______________________________

Inquiry and Decision Making

Directions: Read the following information about an imaginary public policy issue. Use it with what you already know to complete the tasks that follow. You should take about 20 minutes to complete both Task I and Task II. Task I is a selected-response item and Task II is an extended-response item.

A CURFEW IS PROPOSED

A curfew is a time after which people are not allowed to be out on the streets or in public places. Your city council is debating whether to pass the following "youth curfew":

> *All persons under age 17 are prohibited from being in the streets or other public places without an adult from 10 p.m. to 5 a.m. on Sundays through Thursdays during the school year. At all other times, persons under 17 without an adult shall be prohibited from being in the streets or other public places from midnight until 5 a.m.*

PART A In considering their decision, the city council was provided with the following information:

DATA SECTION

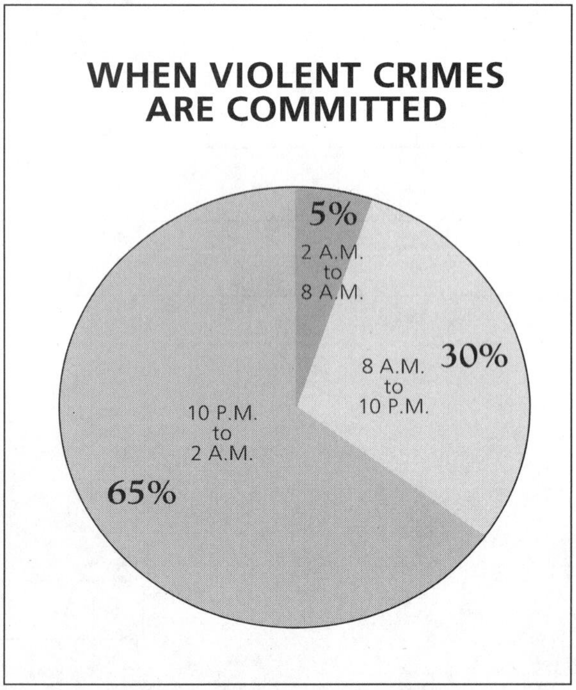

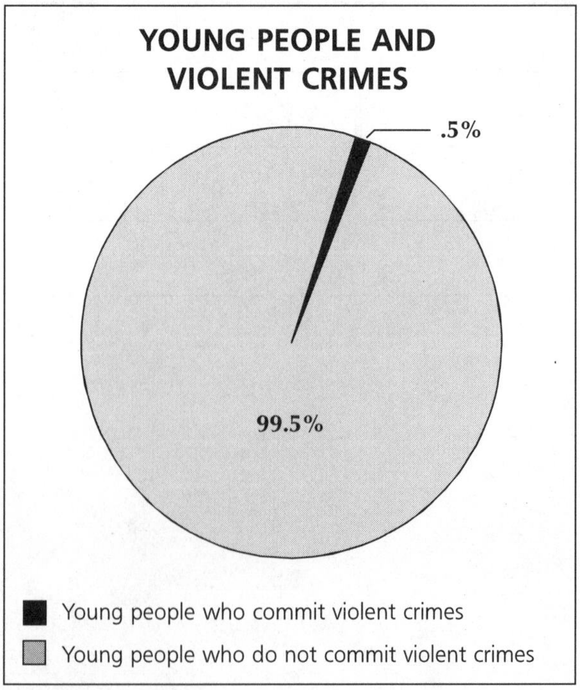

Inquiry and Decision Making

PART B During the city council hearings, the following statements were considered.

Statement #1:
"Ladies and gentlemen, a youth curfew would have serious economic consequences for our community. I say this because in my meetings with other business owners it has become clear that such a curfew would dramatically reduce our sales to teenagers, who are some of our best customers."
John McBain, Owner
Ann Arbor Record Shop

Statement #2:
"We must teach our children to be good citizens. We must continue to promote order and discipline, supporting communities that introduce school uniforms, impose curfews, enforce truancy laws, remove disruptive students from the classroom, and have zero tolerance for guns and drugs in school."
President Bill Clinton
1997 State of the Union Address

COMPLETE THE FOLLOWING TASKS:

Task I: Interpreting Information

23 Study the information in the Data Section. Which of the following statements best describes the *relationship* between **violent crimes** and **times of the day**? Be sure to mark your answer on the answer sheet.

A Most violent crimes are committed by young people.
B Most violent crimes are committed during daylight hours.
C Most violent crimes are committed at night.
D Most violent crimes are committed on weekends.

Task II: Taking a Stand

24 You will now take a stand on the following public issue: **Should the city council pass a curfew limiting the hours young people can be out at night?** You may either support or oppose the curfew. Write a letter to the city council. Use information to provide reasons that support your position.

You will be graded on the following, so be sure your letter includes each of the elements listed below:

- A clear statement of your position.
- Supporting information using core democratic values of American constitutional democracy. (See page 134 for examples.)
- Supporting knowledge from history, geography, civics, or economics that you already know. *(It is not enough to state only your opinion.)*
- Supporting information from the Data Section.

Inquiry and Decision Making

Remember to: Use complete sentences.
Explain your reasons in detail.
Write or print neatly on the lines provided below.

Should the city council pass a curfew limiting the hours young people can be out at night?

Dear Members of the City Council:

STOP

Use this checklist to review your letter.

- ❑ I stated my position clearly.
- ❑ I supported my position with reference to at least one core democratic value of American constitutional democracy.
- ❑ I supported my position with knowledge from history, geography, civics, or economics that I already knew.
- ❑ I supported my position with information from the Data Section.

Name ____________________ Teacher ____________________

Day Two: Social Studies Assessment

Instructions to the Student

There are three types of questions on this test: **selected-response, constructed-response**, and **extended-response**.

- **Selected-response** questions will ask you first to read a passage, map, chart, or table. After studying this prompt, read the questions and choose the best answer from among four answer choices.
- **Constructed-response** questions will ask you to explain a conclusion, provide examples, complete a chart, interpret information, or give a reason for an answer you have given.
- **Extended-response** questions require you to write an answer that is more detailed and requires more thinking. These items ask you to interpret information from a set of data on an imaginary policy issue, identify a relationship presented in the Data Section, take a position for or against the policy, and give reasons supporting your position.

Use the separate answer sheet to mark your choice for the **selected-response** questions. Fill in the circle for your choice on the answer sheet. Remember to fill in the circle completely and cleanly, erasing any stray lines or marks.

Space is provided in the test section for you to write your answers to **constructed-response** and **extended-response** items.

Read all directions for these items carefully.

If you finish early, you may check your work for Day Two **only**. Do **not** work on the Day One section of this test.

Civics

Directions: Examine the following illustration and use it with what you already know to answer the questions that follow:

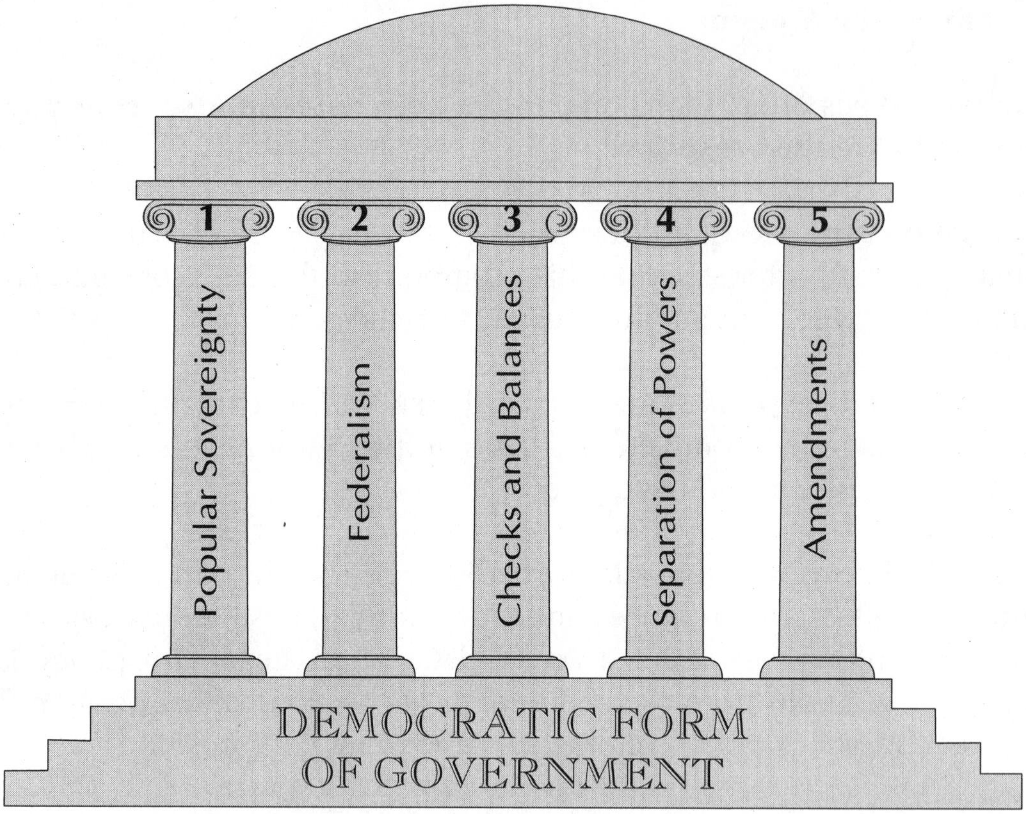

25 What characteristic do all of the columns have in common?

- **A** they limit the power of the national government
- **B** they increase the power of the President of the United States
- **C** they allow the Supreme Court the power to declare laws unconstitutional
- **D** they create a two house legislature

III.1.MS.4

26 Which statement BEST reflects the principle in Column 2?

- **A** The national goverment shares power with 50 state governments.
- **B** The President is Commander-in-Chief of all U.S. Armed Forces
- **C** The U.S. Supreme Court can declare laws to be unconstitutional.
- **D** The Bill of Rights protects individual rights and freedoms.

III.2.MS.2

27 When the President of the United States vetoes a bill passed by the U.S. Congress, it is an example of which principle in action?

- **A** Column 1
- **B** Column 2
- **C** Column 3
- **D** Column 4

III.2.MS.2

28 The ideas found in Column 1 are best reflected by the fact that the

- **A** Bill of Rights was added to the U.S. Constitution
- **B** President can veto an act of the U.S. Congress
- **C** national government controls trade between the states
- **D** U.S. Constitution begins with the words, "We, the people"

III.1.MS.4

29 In which document can ALL of the principles listed on the columns be found?

- **A** Declaration of Independence
- **B** Articles of Confederation
- **C** U.S. Constitution
- **D** Bill of Rights

III.2.MS.2

Civics

Directions: Read the following statements by candidates and use them with what you already know to answer the questions that follow.

CAMPAIGN COMMENTS

The following statements were made by candidates running for office in the last election.

Candidate A: Our elderly population is one of the fastest growing segments of our community. If I am elected I will increase funding to help senior citizens throughout our nation.

Candidate B: I think that our most serious problems are economic ones. If I am elected, I will reduce income taxes, encourage government spending, and reduce business taxes.

Candidate C: I agree that our main challenge is the economy. The problem is that we are losing too many jobs to other countries. If I am elected, I will place a tariff on all foreign goods coming into our country.

Candidate D: Even more important than our economy is our position in the world community. Our nation is a leader in the world. We must live up to our obligations as an international leader.

30 Which tax would MOST likely rise if Candidate A is elected?

A property tax **C** social security tax
B gasoline tax **D** sales tax

III.4.MS.1

31 Which candidate probably would oppose the North American Free Trade Agreement (NAFTA)?

A Candidate A
B Candidate B
C Candidate C
D Candidate D

III.2.MS.3

32 If there were a conflict between two foreign countries, which international organization might Candidate D recommend to settle the dispute?

A Commonwealth of Independent States
B United Nations
C North Atlantic Treaty Organization
D European Union

III.5.MS.2

33 Assuming that these candidates are running for the same elected office, which office is it?

A U.S. Senator from Michigan
B Governor of Michigan
C Mayor of Detroit
D Police Commissioner of Flint

III.2.MS.3

34 Which core democratic value is BEST demonstrated by this election campaign?

A patriotism
B representative government
C checks and balances
D rule of law

III.1.MS.2

Civics

Directions: Examine the following newspaper headlines and use them with what you already know to answer the questions that follow.

THE DAILY NEWS
TENSIONS RISE BETWEEN INDIA AND PAKISTAN; MANY FEAR POSSIBLE WAR

THE DETROIT FREE PRESS
IRAN THREATENS TO CUT OIL SUPPLIES TO THE WEST

THE WORLD TRIBUNE
FRANCE, ITALY AND GERMANY MEET TO DISCUSS TRADE AGREEMENT

35 Select **one** newspaper headline. On the lines provided, identify and describe an international organization that might help handle the situation stated in the headline, and describe the purpose of that organization.

Identification of an international organization that might help handle the situation:

____

Description of the purpose of the organization: ____________________

____

____

____

____

____

____

____

____

____

____

____

____

III.5.MS.1

Name ____________________ Teacher ____________________

Economics

Directions: Read the following chart and use it with what you already know to answer the questions that follow.

ECONOMIC SYSTEMS

COUNTRY 1. In this country people produce what they need by doing things the way they were done in the past. People hunt for food or grow it themselves. A person's role in society is determined at birth.

COUNTRY 2. In this country, all important decisions are made by the king and queen. They hold almost complete power over the political and economic life of their nation. The royal government owns all the land, natural resources, and factories.

COUNTRY 3. In this industrialized country, people are free to produce whatever they wish and to consume whatever they can afford. People produce and sell goods and services in order to make a profit.

COUNTRY 4. Although largely desert, this country contains a vast amount of oil. These oil reserves provide a great source of wealth for the nation. Political power is held by the members of a small ruling family.

Economics

36 What are two basic occupations commonly found in Country 1?

- **A** farming small plots of land and hunting game
- **B** large-scale farming and high technology occupations
- **C** mining and fishing
- **D** white-collar workers and computer technicians

IV.4.MS.1

37 Which country MOST relies on exporting its natural resources to obtain goods and services from other countries?

- **A** Country 1
- **B** Country 2
- **C** Country 3
- **D** Country 4

IV.5.MS.1

38 Which describes an economic situation you would MOST likely find in Country 1?

- **A** there is a thriving import and export business
- **B** there are many computer-related businesses
- **C** people use barter as a common means of payment
- **D** most people are highly skilled and educated

IV.5.MS.3

39 What characteristic do all of the economies in the chart share?

- **A** They all must deal with the problem of scarcity.
- **B** They all are command economies.
- **C** They all rely on computer technology.
- **D** The interaction of supply and demand determines prices.

IV.4.MS.1

40 The economies of the United States, Mexico, Japan, Germany, and Canada most resemble the economy of which country in the chart?

- **A** Country 1
- **B** Country 2
- **C** Country 3
- **D** Country 4

IV.4.MS.1

Economics

Directions: Read the following two advertisements and use them with what you already know to answer the questions that follow.

DONUTS GALORE, INC.

FRESH MADE DONUTS

~~$2.99~~

$1.99 A DOZEN

DAY-OLD DONUTS

89¢ A DOZEN

THE DONUT SHOP

FRESH MADE DONUTS

$2.49 A DOZEN

Economics

41 What would BEST explain why Donuts Galore lowered the price of their donuts to $1.99 a dozen?

A to decrease their income taxes
B to increase their competitiveness
C to increase their sales force
D to decrease production costs

IV.1.MS.1

42 What would be the MOST likely response by The Donut Shop to the action of Donuts Galore?

A decrease their price for donuts
B increase their sales force
C increase their price for donuts
D decrease their advertising

IV.1.MS.1

43 Based on the two advertisements, in which type of economic system do the two donut shops operate?

A a traditional economy
B a command economy
C a free market economy
D an agricultural economy

IV.1.MS.1

44 If state government were to place a special tax on the sale of donuts, what would be the MOST likely effect on both donut shops?

A an increase in donut sales
B an increase in the number of workers needed
C a decrease in donut sales
D a decrease in the cost of doing business

IV.2.MS.3

45 Sugar is an important ingredient in making donuts. If the national government were to lower tariffs on sugar imports to the United States, what would be the most likely effect on the two donut shops?

A decrease production costs
B increase donut sales overseas
C increase production costs
D increase the price of donuts

IV.5.MS.2

Economics

Directions: Examine the following letter and use it with what you already know to complete this task.

Dear Ms. Jones,

Our state is faced with raising additional money to balance the state's budget. I know that you and other Senators in our state legislature are considering a bill to increase taxes.

I have read in the newspaper that the legislature is considering several possible tax increases. The state legislature is considering raising the sales tax, state income tax, or property tax.

I would like to hear from you about your views on which tax you prefer to raise.

Sincerely,

Susan Samms

Economics

46 On the lines provided, select **one** tax described in the letter. Describe how this tax works and explain how one group in society would be affected by an increase in this tax.

Type of tax selected: ______________________________

Description of the tax: ______________________________

____

____

____

How one group in society would be affected by an increase in this tax: ____

____

____

____

____

____

IV.3.MS.4

Name ______________________ Teacher ______________________

Inquiry

Directions: You should take about five minutes to study the following table and use it with what you already know to complete these tasks.

URBANIZATION OF WORLD POPULATIONS

Over the last century, there has been an increasing shift in where people live. This trend is expect to continue.

A SHIFTING WORLD POPULATION

Place	**1900** % of world population	**2050** (estimated) % of world population
Cities of 1 million or more	1.6%	27.1%
Cities of less than 1 million	12.0%	35.4%
Rural Areas	86.4%	37.5%

Task I:

47 Based on the table, make a statement about the relationship between **date** and **where people have lived and will live.**

____

____

V.1.MS.1

Task II:

48 Use information from the table above to make two pie charts showing where people have lived and will live in the two different years. In addition, correctly label each category. (Note: Each space equals 5%.)

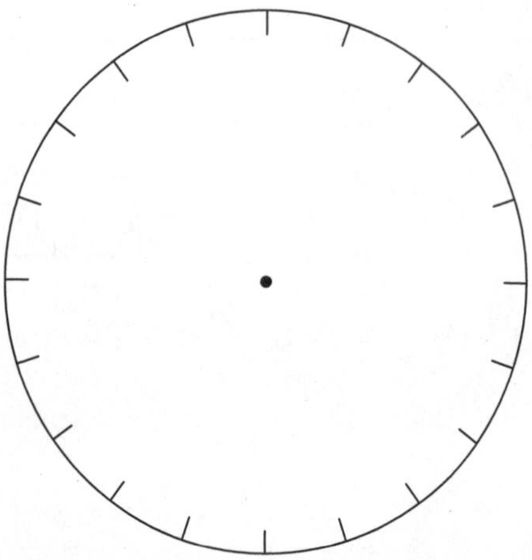

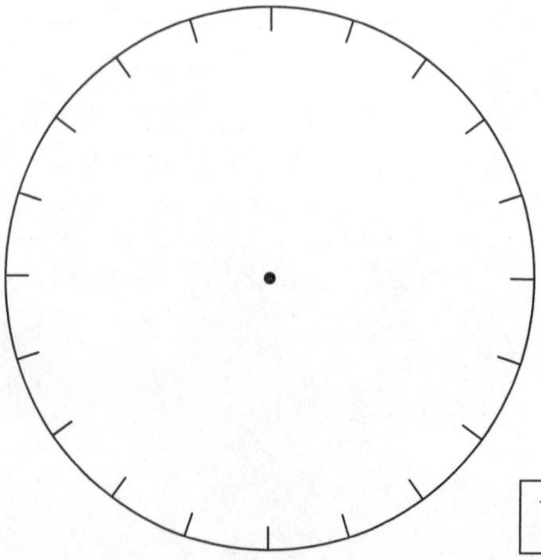

V.1.MS.2

Name ______________________ Teacher ______________________

Inquiry and Decision Making

Directions: Read the following information about an imaginary public policy issue. Use it with what you already know to complete the tasks that follow. You should take about 20 minutes to complete both Task I and Task II. Task I is a selected-response item and Task II is an extended-response item.

YOUR CITY IS CONSIDERING A SELECTIVE BUYING RULE

Country X has a record of human rights abuses — citizens put in jail without a trial for criticizing the government, and prisoners beaten and tortured in violation of international law. Your city council is considering a "selective buying" rule that would prohibit city agencies from doing business with Country X. Your city would also refuse to deal with any firm that does business with Country X, including major corporations.

DATA SECTION

PART A In considering their decision, the city council was provided with the following information about other cities that have already passed similar rules against doing business with Country X:

LOCATION	UNEMPLOYMENT RATE SINCE RULE WAS PASSED
San Francisco, California	increased by 1.0%
Oakland, California	increased by 1.5%
Boulder, Colorado	decreased by 2.1%
Chapel Hill, North Carolina	increased by 3.1%
New York City, New York	increased by 1.8%

PART B During the city council hearings, the following testimony was heard.

"I doubt this rule can bring about any change in Country X's policy. We conducted a study of 100 similar selective buying rules. We found that such rules almost never cause a country to change its ways. We also believe that such a rule will increase our cost of doing business by forcing us to buy from companies that charge higher prices."

President, Foreign Trade Business Council

"I beg you to approve this rule. My organization believes it will force Country X to end its human rights abuses. During the 1980s, many American cities passed laws against buying from companies with ties to South Africa. This eventually forced South Africa to end its policy of racial discrimination, proving such rules can be successful."

President, Concerned Citizens

Inquiry and Decision Making

COMPLETE THE FOLLOWING TASKS:

Task I: Interpreting Information

49 Study the information in the Data Section. Which of the following statements best describes the *relationship* between **cities with a selective buying rule** and **rates of unemployment**? Be sure to mark your answer on the answer sheet.

A Cities with a selective buying rule generally had decreased unemployment rates.

B Cities located on the west coast of the United States had their unemployment rates rise the most because of the selective buying rule.

C There was no change in the unemployment rate for cities that adopted a selective buying rule.

D Unemployment rates tended to increase in cities with a selective buying rule.

Task II: Taking a Stand

50 You will now take a stand on the following public issue: **Should the city council pass a selective buying rule against Country X?** You may either support or oppose the buying rule. Write a letter to the city council. Use information to provide reasons that support your position.

You will be graded on the following, so be sure your letter includes each of the elements listed below:

- A clear statement of your position.
- Supporting information using core democratic values of American constitutional democracy. (See page 134 for examples.)
- Supporting knowledge from history, geography, civics, or economics that you already know. *(It is not enough to state only your opinion.)*
- Supporting information from the Data Section.

Remember to: Use complete sentences.
Explain your reasons in detail.
Write or print neatly on the lines provided.

Inquiry and Decision Making

Should the city council pass a selective buying rule against Country X?

Dear City Council Members:

continued...

Name ______________________ Teacher ______________________

Use this checklist to review your letter.

- ❑ I stated my position clearly.
- ❑ I supported my position with reference to at least one core democratic value of American constitutional democracy.
- ❑ I supported my position with knowledge from history, geography, civics, or economics that I already knew.
- ❑ I supported my position with information from the Data Section.

INDEX

ANSWER SHEET FOR SELECTED-RESPONSE QUESTIONS IN PRACTICE SOCIAL STUDIES MEAP TEST, GRADE 8

Student______________________ Class______________________

Teacher______________________ Date______________________

DAY ONE

GEOGRAPHY					HISTORY				
1	Ⓐ	Ⓑ	Ⓒ	Ⓓ	12	Ⓐ	Ⓑ	Ⓒ	Ⓓ
2	Ⓐ	Ⓑ	Ⓒ	Ⓓ	13	Ⓐ	Ⓑ	Ⓒ	Ⓓ
3	Ⓐ	Ⓑ	Ⓒ	Ⓓ	14	Ⓐ	Ⓑ	Ⓒ	Ⓓ
4	Ⓐ	Ⓑ	Ⓒ	Ⓓ	15	Ⓐ	Ⓑ	Ⓒ	Ⓓ
5	Ⓐ	Ⓑ	Ⓒ	Ⓓ	16	Ⓐ	Ⓑ	Ⓒ	Ⓓ
6	Ⓐ	Ⓑ	Ⓒ	Ⓓ	17	Ⓐ	Ⓑ	Ⓒ	Ⓓ
7	Ⓐ	Ⓑ	Ⓒ	Ⓓ	18	Ⓐ	Ⓑ	Ⓒ	Ⓓ
8	Ⓐ	Ⓑ	Ⓒ	Ⓓ	19	Ⓐ	Ⓑ	Ⓒ	Ⓓ
9	Ⓐ	Ⓑ	Ⓒ	Ⓓ	20	Ⓐ	Ⓑ	Ⓒ	Ⓓ
10	Ⓐ	Ⓑ	Ⓒ	Ⓓ	21	Ⓐ	Ⓑ	Ⓒ	Ⓓ

INQUIRY AND DECISION MAKING				
23	Ⓐ	Ⓑ	Ⓒ	Ⓓ

DAY TWO

CIVICS					ECONOMICS				
25	Ⓐ	Ⓑ	Ⓒ	Ⓓ	36	Ⓐ	Ⓑ	Ⓒ	Ⓓ
26	Ⓐ	Ⓑ	Ⓒ	Ⓓ	37	Ⓐ	Ⓑ	Ⓒ	Ⓓ
27	Ⓐ	Ⓑ	Ⓒ	Ⓓ	38	Ⓐ	Ⓑ	Ⓒ	Ⓓ
28	Ⓐ	Ⓑ	Ⓒ	Ⓓ	39	Ⓐ	Ⓑ	Ⓒ	Ⓓ
29	Ⓐ	Ⓑ	Ⓒ	Ⓓ	40	Ⓐ	Ⓑ	Ⓒ	Ⓓ
30	Ⓐ	Ⓑ	Ⓒ	Ⓓ	41	Ⓐ	Ⓑ	Ⓒ	Ⓓ
31	Ⓐ	Ⓑ	Ⓒ	Ⓓ	42	Ⓐ	Ⓑ	Ⓒ	Ⓓ
32	Ⓐ	Ⓑ	Ⓒ	Ⓓ	43	Ⓐ	Ⓑ	Ⓒ	Ⓓ
33	Ⓐ	Ⓑ	Ⓒ	Ⓓ	44	Ⓐ	Ⓑ	Ⓒ	Ⓓ
34	Ⓐ	Ⓑ	Ⓒ	Ⓓ	45	Ⓐ	Ⓑ	Ⓒ	Ⓓ

INQUIRY AND DECISION MAKING				
49	Ⓐ	Ⓑ	Ⓒ	Ⓓ

NOTES

FORTRAN Programming: A Spiral Approach

Second Edition

Compatible with WATFOR/WATFIV and FORTRAN 77

Charles B. Kreitzberg
Educational Testing Service

Ben Shneiderman
University of Maryland, College Park

Harcourt Brace Jovanovich, Inc.
New York San Diego Chicago San Francisco Atlanta
London Sydney Toronto

To the memory of my father
—C.B.K.

To my wife, Nancy
—B.A.S.

ISBN: 0-15-528015-5

Library of Congress Catalog Number: 81-83981

Printed in the United States of America

CREDITS AND ACKNOWLEDGMENTS
p. 5, top: Photo courtesy of IBM; p. 5, bottom left: Photo courtesy of IBM; p. 5, bottom right: Photo courtesy of IBM; p. 7, top: U.P.I.; p. 7, bottom: Photo courtesy of IBM; p. 8, top: Photo courtesy of IBM; p. 8, bottom: Photo courtesy of IBM.